P9-ECP-438

**MacGregor's Book
Nook Discard**
202 North Main Street
Yreka, CA 96097
(530) 841-2664

DON'T DIE BROKE!

MELVIN JAY SWARTZ

DON'T DIE BROKE!

A Guide to Secure Retirement

MACMILLAN PUBLISHING CO., INC.

NEW YORK

COPYRIGHT © 1975 BY MELVIN JAY SWARTZ

All rights reserved. No part of this book may be reproduced or transmitted in any form or by any means, electronic or mechanical, including photocopying, recording or by any information storage and retrieval system, without permission in writing from the Publisher.

Macmillan Publishing Co., Inc.
866 Third Avenue, New York, N.Y. 10022
Collier-Macmillan Canada Ltd.

Library of Congress Cataloging in Publication Data

Swartz, Melvin Jay.
    Don't die broke!

    1. Aged—Legal status, laws, etc.—United States.
2. Estate planning—United States.   3. Old age
pensions—United States.   I. Title.
KF390.A4S9   340'.02'40565   75-13341
ISBN 0-02-615560-5

First Printing 1975

Printed in the United States of America

*This book is gratefully dedicated to those who
helped me seek some solutions to the problems of
retirement and widowhood—my clients and
colleagues in my retirement community.*

Stuart Skinner
A p r - 5 - 7 6

Contents

CONTENTS   ix

INTRODUCTION

Make Your Retirement Enjoyable

A large number of retired and widowed people are in serious distress. They are annoyed, hounded, and abused. Much of this abuse they bring upon themselves. A surprising number live in fear. Many are depressed. Anxiety prevents them from seeking valid solutions to their problems, and exposes them to profiteers. This situation is as unnecessary as it is bizarre. You can make your retirement enjoyable.

Careful planning and prudent management can minimize the traumas that retirement often brings. A reasonable inquiry is thus in order for those of us who are retiring or retired. Remember that the responsibility of protecting yourself is strictly upon you. Seeking technical advice from just anyone, so long as it is ostensibly "free," invites disaster. Those realtors, mutual funds salesmen, annuity peddlers, and bank employees who act beyond the scope of their expertise cannot help but mislead you. On the other hand, vast, enormous profits motivate the unscrupulous who offer "free" but ultimately expensive advice.

This book is a guide for widows and the retired. It explains wills, trusts, probate (when to avoid it, and when you should not), joint tenancy, and taxes. It also discusses ways to protect your assets, what to do when a spouse dies, and how to avoid legal problems in a second marriage. It provides you with criteria against which decisions can be made. Necessity demands that such discussions be focused on principles. Competent counsel should be sought to advise you on their particular application to your personal needs. This book is designed to help you understand what options are available to you, before and after retirement, so that you can both avoid mistakes and recognize the likelihood of your need for professional advice.

The scope of this book is limited. It does not deal with the psychological, social, and emotional problems of retirement. It does recognize that emotional problems are often caused by a lack of understanding of legal and financial ones. If you don't understand the legal consequences of your acts, it is certainly natural to be upset and depressed, but this situation is not necessary.

Your common problems with Social Security are briefly discussed. Detailed information is available, without charge, from your local Social Security office, which is staffed by competent, helpful employees who will be happy to assist you with any Social Security problems.

This is the first time in modern history that most people can anticipate and look forward to a retirement. Prior to 1930, retirement was only possible for the well-to-do. The Social Security system and the increase in pension and profit-sharing plans made it possible for the average person to consider retirement. The large body of people retired today, therefore, are the first. They are, as it were, the grand experiment.

Many mistakes were made in planning for mass retirements. This was to be expected. It takes time to analyze and improve something new. As time passes, pension and profit-sharing plans will be improved so that the average working individual will not have to lose so much of his hard-earned retirement benefits in modest monthly sums to protect a spouse. Pension and profit-sharing plans will have a cost-of-living increase built in. Federal insurance will be required so that these plans will be guaranteed, and not disappear if a company goes bankrupt. Retirement communities will be better planned. Society will find a way to use the tremendous talents gained by the retired in a lifetime of work experience. There is great hope that retirement in the future will become more valuable to society and more enjoyable to the individual. This does not, however, excuse us from making the best of what we have today.

I do not indulge in the presumption that the average man delights in reading lawyer-like discussions. Throughout this text, layman's language is used whenever possible. Legal terms, if necessary, are explained in simple words.

This book will be of service to those of you who have minimum assets. You cannot afford to lose any of what you have. This book will be of most service to those of you who have substantial assets, for it will show you how to preserve what you own, and perhaps increase your estate. All of you will learn that you are not unique and that you face common problems. The problems are analyzed, and reasonable solutions are suggested.

It is my hope that this book will help you minimize lawyer fees, bank commissions, estate expenses, and taxes after death. Most of all, it is my hope that you will understand how to maximize your income during retirement and not lose your assets while you live.

PART ONE
Before You Retire

1

Plan for Retirement

The goal of this book is to help you enjoy your retirement. You owe it to yourself to do it right and have a good time doing it. You can anticipate many good years if you made it to your early sixties and beyond. New ideas and new concepts are awaiting you. No one has to be a stick-in-the-mud. You need not run out of money. You can keep what you have and perhaps increase your assets. This book goes into all of these things.

You do not have to be lonely, either. You are part of an enormous peer group. There are over twenty-five million of you, and your number is growing. So are your options and choices. You will be around for a long time. Do it right and make it exciting. You just might step into the happiest quarter-century of your life.

Most of us do not plan for retirement or widowhood. It just happens. That is how it was with many of my clients. They graciously discussed with me the emo-

3

tional and financial consequences of uninformed decisions. They told me they had failed to understand their
options and had not known where or when to seek
competent help. We felt there must be an efficient, inexpensive approach to this problem. Planning is a practical start. Plan your retirement well, and it should be
an exhilarating experience which will launch you into
an exciting new age.

Start now. Make checklists for retirement at least a
year in advance. Your checklists should include the following (and anything else that will be essential to your
own personal dream).

1. A complete and detailed analysis of your assets:
   (a) These assets must have a current, valid, realistic
   fair market value. They might include your home and
   its contents, jewelry, nonincome-producing investments, such as group ventures dealing in real estate,
   coin collections, and stamp collections.
2. A list of every source from which you will receive any
   income, such as the following:
   (a) Social Security for you and your spouse.
   (b) Part-time work, if it is in your planning.
   (c) Pension and profit-sharing plans from your employment (list all choices and options).
   (d) All dividends from investments.
   (e) All rents from real estate.
   (f) All income from bank deposits, certificates of deposit, bonds, and the like.
   (g) Consultation in the field in which you have spent
   your life. This is an untapped market for many executives.

3. List in detail your current living expenses. Include approximate current costs of food, medicines, and drugs not covered by insurance; rents; taxes (real estate, estimated income-tax installment payments); general maintenance of your home (repairs and utilities, automobile maintenance, clothing, and all such related items).

Once these lists are completed, start to analyze your financial position. Where can you save money?

Consider such questions as these: Is your home now too large for you and your spouse? Could you sell it at a substantial profit and purchase a smaller, easier to maintain garden apartment, or other, more practical lodging? This might result in small payments or no payments at all. It certainly should minimize your repair and maintenance bills and, perhaps, give you a little additional profit for investment.

Also, is there good reason to buy a new car just because you retired? Your income is going to be limited now. If you need a new car, consider the purchase of a compact.

Many people make common errors. In particular, they don't plan to minimize their general overhead and maximize their income, once retired. For example, a houseful of antiques collected over the years might be sold for a substantial amount of money. If you have an old Tiffany lamp lying around, you could almost retire on that alone. Don't assume your old things are junk. They may have substantial hidden value.

Your new residence may not house all of these things,

and selling them could produce investment capital for you. Look for the most profitable way to amass liquid assets; place these liquid assets into a secure income-producing investment which will slowly grow, hedge against inflation, and also augment your retirement income.

While thinking about investments, if you have any old, inactive savings accounts, check on them at once, especially if you have moved and not changed your address on those accounts. Many states have laws relating to inactive accounts. After so many years of non-use your account might be part of some school fund.

Carefully consider what assets you have that do not produce a fair and reasonable income; perhaps it would be prudent to dispose of them now. Sell them. While you work, you have the income to pay capital gains taxes which might accrue from the sales of these assets.

Eliminate all risk equities from your portfolio. You want to maintain and preserve your assets. Once you retire, it is no longer prudent to risk loss while seeking additional growth. Solidify and maximize your income; learn to live within this income. Once you accept this position, a sense of relief and freedom from worry will make your retirement much more comfortable. There are many conservative, income-producing securities available for the retired.

Do not liquidate all of your assets and put your monies into a nongrowth annuity or savings account. These steps could spell disaster down the road, if inflation continues. You must maintain the dollar value of your principal. You must maintain the purchasing power of your dollar. This is one area where most mistakes are made. Too much cash in savings accounts, thought to be a secure investment, is, in fact, a loss. It is a guaranteed loss. Savings accounts lose money through the ravages of inflation.

This is the first time in your life that you have 100 percent free choice to do whatever you want, whenever you want. It is also the first time you no longer have need to save money. You can and should live on all of your income. It seems foolish that this is such an important statement. However, many retired people continue to save part of their income out of fear or habit. Your income is limited in retirement. You should see that you get the most income available, and then use it all. To do otherwise is wasteful. You not only limit your lifestyle, but you also increase estate costs and estate taxes at death.

Many of my retired clients feel that, when they were younger and healthier, they failed to anticipate medical problems that might come down the road. It is essential that you have a complete physical examination while you are employed and covered by group insurance. If you require any operations in the near future, do it while you are in good health and employed, when you are protected with group medical insurance. Most medical and health insurance policies do not provide 100 percent coverage, but you should still use them to your maximum advantage while they exist.

This is the one area where many of my retired clients most regret the lost opportunity to save money. If they had the chance to do it again, they would all have every medical check-up available while employed. Visit your optometrist, ophthalmologist, and dentist. These are areas where the retired have most of their problems. These services cost more money if they are ignored. Take advantage of any group insurance available to you while you are still employed. Take leave of your employment in the best possible physical condition.

If your medical insurance doesn't cover all of the expenses, take the deductions from your income tax for the bills you pay. If you wait until you have no income to deduct them from, then you will lose 100 percent of the monies you paid for medical expenses. Be sure your physical condition is good *before* you retire. As we get older our nutritional needs change. You might consult a dietitian if you have problems.

You may want to consider moving to a different, perhaps warmer, climate once you retire. At retirement age, there would probably be one, or at best two, of you to consider. Your sons and daughters are probably independent. You are a free agent. Do not burden yourself with the need to live next to your children. They need their freedom. You deserve yours. You can live anywhere in this country and still keep in touch with your family, with today's modern communication and transportation systems. But again, plan carefully.

2

Your Life Insurance

Once you retire, you will probably ask yourself, "How did I get so broke?" Perhaps you will spend too much money, on your limited income. Have you considered all your unnecessary expenses? For example, life insurance can be a trap for the retired.

Do you remember when you first bought your life insurance? You didn't think you could afford it, but social pressure and the persistent salesman convinced you that you had a duty to provide for the education of your children, if you died too soon. Insurance companies still run the same type of advertisement. You also felt you had to protect your wife with insurance because you had nothing else. So you bought that expensive policy and felt good about yourself.

Now, thirty to forty years later, you still have this policy and pay for it out of your retirement income. You should stop to see if the reason for the policy still exists. Certainly the need to raise and educate your children is gone.

The life insurance industry spends millions on advertising to promote the image that to die without life insurance ranks with kicking your mother and stepping on the flag. It does not.

There are many alternatives to life insurance once you retire. To better understand this, it is important to remember why you bought it in the first place years ago. Then, it was probably security for your family, in case you died too soon. If by the time you've retired you still have nothing else—no assets, no stocks, no real estate, no cash or bonds, keep your insurance and go on to the next chapter.

For those of you who have saved, invested, and managed to put something aside, the need for insurance at this stage of your life is questionable.*

There are two common types of insurance. One is term insurance. It has no cash surrender value. It is never paid up, and you must make premium payments for the rest of your life. It is much cheaper than whole life in the beginning, but the premium costs get more expensive as you become older. You can't do much to help your retirement with term policies except terminate them as soon as possible. Most term insurance is purchased for a temporary period, or is bought for a limited and particular purpose, and should not be retained throughout your life.

* The one exception: If you have nonliquid assets and a taxable estate, you might need insurance to pay estate taxes.

6⁰ Dnt put all assets into a non
growth annuity or saving
act.
9. Life ins. can b. a tsap for
return

The other type of insurance is called whole life insurance. It costs the most and pays the highest commissions. If you are imprudent and plan to keep your policy forever, this is probably the kind to buy. When you buy a whole life insurance policy, a small, indeed a most modest stipend is put aside by the insurance company for you out of each premium payment. You own this money. It is called the cash surrender value. Most companies do not pay any interest to you for keeping and using your money. This type of insurance is sold with the sales pitch that your money is available for an emergency. Retirement is your emergency. You want to increase your retirement income.

There is often a better and less expensive way to provide money for your spouse, without additional loss through inflation, which is inevitable with insurance. You might also be able to receive some benefit from the intelligent use of your insurance monies while you live.

Many of you don't realize that if you have a fifty-thousand-dollar, thirty- to forty-year-old life insurance policy, you probably have close to a $25,000 cash surrender value in that policy by the time you retire. How many of you have inquired to find out just how much you do have? Why not do it now? That money is yours; you own it. If you terminate the policy, you can take that money out now and invest it in a conservative income-producing investment. In addition, you will not be paying premiums out of your limited retirement income.

If you are concerned about your health, and do not

want to terminate the policy, you can still use the cash surrender money. You can borrow this money from the insurance company at an interest rate that is usually less than bank rates, and invest it. You will also be able to deduct the interest payments from your income tax.

You want to improve your retirement income. You do not want to spend your reduced and limited income paying premiums for something you do not really need. Your old policy should have a substantial built-up cash surrender value. If you can't bring yourself to take this money and terminate the policy, at least use your cash surrender value to buy a paid-up policy, and don't waste any more of your income on premiums. However, I consider this a last resort, and a bad waste of money.

Make a list of all insurance policies you own today. Analyze them with an estate planner, such as an estate tax lawyer, to see if you can convert these policies to your advantage. Your insurance agent is *nct* the expert to do this for you. He will lose commissions if you terminate your policies.

Don't forget: You purchased the insurance to protect your family in case of premature death. Now your children are grown, educated, and off with their own families. They do not need your life insurance. Neither do you! You also don't receive any benefit from these policies or this money while you live; neither does your wife. By the time you die, inflation will shrink this policy to a fraction of its true value.

If you decide you don't need the insurance blanket, and have the courage to turn it in and take your cash surrender value, you will immediately increase your retirement income.

Remember: $25,000' worth of cash surrender value out of your insurance, producing a normal 6 percent income a year from a conservative investment, could give you an additional $1,500 a year spending money in the form of income. This is nothing to sneeze at! Obviously, it is more if your cash surrender value is more. Some of this extra income might even be tax-exempt. Your broker can assist you here. In addition to the added income you now receive, you will save the money you otherwise might have spent to make annual or semiannual premium payments. So, in reality, you will not only increase your spendable income during retirement by $1,500, but you also will have additional income to spend, which otherwise would have paid for the insurance premiums. Most important, your former insurance money will not shrink in value through inflation.

All insurance policies must depreciate in value daily. They shrink as a result of inflation. The money has much less purchasing power for your heirs when you die. These policies should not be held longer than is absolutely necessary. Once you retire, the insurance gives you no advantage. (One exception, of course, is if you have a nonliquid taxable estate for which you might need insurance for tax purposes.) Once you retire, the vast majority of you receive no advantage from life insurance. You have long lost the need for an insurance blanket.

Many people don't realize that if you have a life insurance policy that will pay approximately $50,000 on your death, by the time you reach retirement age you will have a cash surrender value of approximately $25,000. If you die, and the policy pays the $50,000 face, insured amount, you do not receive the cash surrender value money in addition to the $50,000. In other words, the $25,000 cash surrender value is lost. It is retained by the insurance company, so in effect, they do not pay you $50,000. They pay your heirs $25,000 plus the $25,000 which is yours before you die to make the total of $50,000. This is one area of great abuse by insurance companies. The day before you die, you can take that $25,000 out. The day after you die, it is lost to you. This should tell you something about economics. It would be so much more prudent to take that money which is yours now. If you need additional insurance, buy cheap term insurance. Many of you are retiring younger these days, at 60 to 65. If you are in good health, you can still buy term life insurance on your life. Term life insurance does not have the cash surrender value which, by the way, pays a minimum interest. However, you no longer need that cash surrender value money to be retained by the insurance company. When you think that the insurance company pays your beneficiary not $50,000 of their money at your death, but $25,000 of their money and $25,000 of your money, why should you want to continue to pay premiums for a $50,000 policy? You should take your cash surrender value, turn in your policies and invest this cash. Twenty-five thousand dollars' worth of investible money in the most conservative investment will still pay you approximately $1,500 a year. The $25,000 which you took out from your old insurance will, no doubt, grow over the years, hedge against inflation, and be worth more than $25,000 by the time you die.

Many employers have term life insurance policies on their former employees. This type of insurance has no cash surrender value. If you don't make the annual payments on the premiums, by all means keep this insurance. It is possible today to increase your advantage with that policy, also. Most of you named your spouse as first beneficiary and your children as alternate beneficiaries on that company policy. This is good! Today, however, you can also make these individuals the *owners* of that policy. This is very important for term insurance.

The same office that manages the retirement section of your company usually handles the insurance. Write and ask for a change-of-ownership form. Tell them you wish to make your spouse the *owner* of the policy, as well as the beneficiary, or, of course, your children, if you have no spouse. This simple little maneuver will remove the total value of that term insurance from your potential taxable estate at death. You can save your family substantial estate taxes in this manner.

Be very careful! Do not transfer the ownership of your regular, *whole* life insurance that has a built-up cash surrender value, without expert tax advice. You might incur gift taxes if you do. Any advice given here should be carefully checked with a competent counselor to make the proper adaptation to your own needs.

In addition, if you retire your life insurance without expert advice, you might in the rare instance suffer a small income-tax liability. I don't wish to become too technical at this point, and I don't wish to prevent you from cashing in the insurance. Most of you can cash in your insurance policies without any liabilities. If there is a modest income tax, which might fall due, this should be analyzed by an expert. In any event, the tax is usually *most* modest.

Discussions herein on technical areas, such as taxes (gift, estate, inheritance, and income taxes), estate planning, law, and so on, must, of course, by their very nature be presented in a very simplified manner. You should seek the advice of an estate attorney for your own particular needs. This is not the area for self-help. Most laymen do not have the knowledge to handle these affairs without competent assistance. Regrettably, your insurance agent is not the proper expert in this instance. He will be happy to assist you—if he can convince you to immediately purchase an annuity. Don't do it. Most annuities are absurd. You would be well advised to ignore the advertisements that scream at you, "How would you like a guaranteed income for life?" You might as well keep the insurance, for all of the advantage you receive from annuities. They are every bit as bad as savings accounts, if not worse. Both depreciate constantly, daily, through inflation.

If you have not already done so, it is most important to examine and review all your insurance policies immediately. No matter what kind of insurance you have, be sure to give your beneficiaries all of the insurance in one lump-sum payment at your death. It is downright imprudent and humiliating not to. When you limit your spouse to monthly payments, he or she loses money. The insurance companies earn huge amounts of income from your money, which they often hold without paying any interest or, at best, the most minimum interest. The monthly payments are ridiculously small. Their buying power decreases daily through inflation. Your spouse and children also lose any possible chance of growth or investment with this money. All growth investment and increased values are retained by the insurance company.

Make sure your policies read "Option One," which is usually the option referring to lump-sum payment. Look for the words, "One Lump-Sum Payment," and circle that choice. If you are not sure, your insurance agent should assist you in making the proper choice. Your spouse can then purchase a conservative investment, as previously mentioned, with this money. More often than not, the income earned by the conservative stock will exceed the monthly payments paid by most insurance companies. In any event, the purchasing power of your dollar will not be decreased daily. I cannot emphasize too strongly the absurdity in allowing the companies to hold your money and use it for nothing.

3

Your Expert Adviser

You would be well advised to seek an attorney in your community whose practice is substantially limited to tax-estate planning. There are lawyers in every community who specialize in, or limit their practice to this field. You can ask the attorney if he is a member of the "Estate Planning Council" in his community. If he is not, you can assume he is not truly a full-time estate planner.

There is a book you can refer to, in most public libraries, titled *Sullivan's Probate Directory*. This book lists law firms or attorneys in every community in the United States that has more than 25,000 residents. The firm or attorney listed has been rated in that community, by his colleagues, as an estate-planning specialist.

This is a very simple way to find your expert. The fee you pay for expert advice will save large amounts of money and make your retirement substantially more comfortable.

Your attorney does not earn commissions. He is not interested in selling you expensive 8 percent commissioned mutual funds (which the retired should not buy, anyway). He will not sell you a trust if the yearly cost of the trust will be too expensive for the services received. He should not be interested in anything, except serving you at a reasonable hourly fee. Your interest is his interest. There should be no hidden profits for him.

The best advice I can give you is to encourage you to find yourself a good tax-estate-planning attorney to help you with your retirement plans. You will need a proper estate plan and a will. Wills that are more than five years old are often expensive to use and usually do not reflect your most recent wishes. If a living trust is advisable, the attorney is the person to assist you. Your personal counsel will analyze that picture with you. A later part on trusts discusses this subject in depth, and will help you understand your lawyer's advice.

Once you find your expert, ask him or her to analyze your insurance with you to see if the terminating of the coverage is worthwhile. This attorney can also help you make the proper choice on your pension or profit-sharing plan. If you have listed your assets, analyzed your position, and understand the concepts in this book, you will be able to discuss your options intelligently at that time.

There is a regrettable problem in my retirement community and, I understand, in some others. Most retirees who move to these retirement communities have no local sources of reference when they seek an attorney.

They are invited into the Trust Department of a local bank where a trust officer is "alleged" to interview them. He then recommends a local attorney. Unfortunately, trust officers in some banks in some retirement communities recommend the same three or four lawyers. The three or four lawyers were, until quite recently, trust officers in these banks. Those to whom I refer left their bank positions as trust officers to practice law and established quite successful practices quickly, which is quite remarkable. It would appear that there is a painful private relationship between some bank trust officers in some retirement communities and these former bank employees or ex-trust officers. The present trust officers recommend their former associates who recommend what the bank wants to the clients. One might question why such a relationship exists. The bank will reward the former trust officers when your estate is administered, by hiring them and paying them legal fees when they administer your estate. There are a number of competent attorneys in all communities. You must protect yourself by asking why some of these trust departments seem to limit their recommendations to their former colleagues. You can demand that they recommend all the competent lawyers in your community, even those who were not former trust officers.

4

The Pension Plan

In my opinion, after insurance, the second most abused area for the retired concerns advice about choosing the retirement plan offered by your company. The executive in charge of these plans is, first, a company person, whose interest lies in protecting the company as much as in protecting you. You must recognize realistically that some people who offer advice might have ulterior motives. We must analyze this motivation before we seek or follow their advice.

Most corporate attorneys are employees of the corporation and are very competent. Nevertheless, they are competent corporation and business attorneys. Generally, their knowledge of estate planning and taxes is zero! Generally, their knowledge of retirement problems is *less* than zero! They may well know less about these problems than you. Seeking advice from such a person is a perfect example of the blind leading the blind.

In your pre-retirement year, you should analyze all the options in your particular retirement plan. Most corporations which offer retirement plans have three or more choices:

1. Generally, under the first you receive 100 percent of all of your retirement benefits in the form of monthly income. This income stops at your death.

2. The second option usually offers something like 75 percent to you, and approximately 25 percent—and sometimes slightly more—to your spouse in monthly annuity payments, once you die.

3. Under the third plan, you take 50 percent of your total income, and if you die before your spouse, 50 percent will be paid monthly to him or her after your death.

Most of my clients choose plan three. What an absurdity! If your spouse dies first, you never get more than that 50 percent. Choosing a retirement plan is no time to become emotional. It is not the time to feel you must do what others think would be right. This is the time to analyze what your income will be during retirement, and opt for the maximum income.

Most corporations have millions of dollars in unused assets (tax free), in the form of pension and profit-sharing plans. The greatest increase these plans enjoy comes when individuals give up half their justly earned monies. This is an outrage! Perhaps, someday, some congressional committee will rectify this abuse, but in the interim, you must protect yourself!

Generally speaking, if you are not five years or so

older than your spouse, you should not automatically take the smallest income in an attempt to protect him or her after your death. There are many other factors to consider, before you make a choice. Here are some of them:

1. Does your spouse have separate assets?

2. Does your spouse also have a pension or profit-sharing plan from working?

3. Will your spouse inherit anything from someone else?

4. If your spouse is sick and your health is good, his or her life expectancy might be substantially less than yours. Why would you want to give up half of your income to protect him or her under these circumstances?

5. If you are both healthy and you retire young enough to still be insurable, you might consider an additional alternative, but only as a last choice. Find a life insurance agent and ask him how much term life insurance you can buy with an amount of money *equal* to what you would have let the company keep, if you take less than 100 percent of your retirement income.

I am not advocating here something inconsistent with my statements in Chapter 2 where you were advised to consider terminating your insurance. This is an entirely different situation. This is a matter of economic choices. You must take a cold, hard look at your alternatives at this point.

You might be in a better position to take 100 percent of your retirement benefits and use some of that money to purchase "term insurance" on your life to protect your spouse if you die first and want additional assets for him or her.

Your old life insurance policy, the one that I suggested terminating, had the built-up cash surrender value. That is worth cash to you today. You can use that cash for income-producing investments. If you feel the need to protect your spouse further or don't have sufficient assets if you die, you might want to purchase term insurance. As far as the old insurance, which I discussed in Chapter 2, is concerned, many of you had whole-life insurance. Throughout your working years, as you paid your premiums on the old policy, a small—indeed, a most modest—stipend was put aside by the insurance company for you. Many policies were sold with a sales pitch stating that your money is available any time for an emergency. Retirement is your emergency. You want to improve your retirement position. For example, if you have a $30,000 life insurance policy on which you paid premiums throughout your working years, that policy should have a substantial cash surrender value of about $15,000. You can turn in the policy and take out $15,000 in cash. If you die with that policy, your beneficiary does not receive the $30,000 face value plus the cash surrender value money. That cash surrender value money is lost. The insurance company keeps that $15,000 without so much as a thank you. The cash surrender value is sort of a here-today-and-gone-tomorrow thing. Most people lose it happily through ignorance. This does not make sense. Take that money which is rightfully yours.

Of course, you want to protect your spouse. We all want to do this. If you are in good health, you can buy a substantial life insurance policy with that half of your retirement income which you otherwise would have let your company keep (to carry on after your death for your wife, if she be still alive). At your death, the new term insurance policy could mean a handful of cash for your spouse, who could then use the insurance money to purchase an additional income-producing utility stock or bond. This might well produce more income for him or her than the continued 50 percent of your retirement income, which would have depreciated annually in its purchasing power through inflation. All fixed incomes from pension plans constantly depreciate. Their purchasing power is less every single year. Very few pension plans have a cost of living increase factor built into them. Very few of them will pay more as the cost of living increases. If your spouse is to maintain his or her standard of living, it is essential that you help him or her find a way to beat the inflation factor.

For example, if that portion of your retirement which you would have left with your company can purchase you a term life insurance policy in the amount of $30,000 or more, you will not lose anything by cashing it in; rather, you can probably make substantial gains for your family. You were willing to take a loss in retirement income to protect your spouse, but there might be a better way. For instance, you take 100 percent of your retirement income, but only live on the amount you would have received if you had taken a lesser plan. Ask your life insurance agent to find out how much term life insurance you can buy with the amount of money you otherwise would have let your company keep. In other words, you will not *use* all of your 100 percent retirement income. Use that portion of the income which you would have let the company keep to make payments on a new term insurance policy on your life. You will not receive anything less than you would have received had you taken less than what you earned. You might gain a lot more for your entire family thus:

1. If you are in good health, you might be able to purchase a modest life insurance policy with that half of your retirement income which you otherwise would have let the company keep. At your death, that policy means a handful of cash for your spouse. Your spouse could then use the insurance monies to purchase an additional income-producing utility stock or bond. This might well produce more income than the continued 50 percent of your retirement pension.

2. This is a method whereby you can greatly increase your estate without spending any of your own money. If you had taken less than 100 percent benefits under your retirement plan, your children would receive nothing from it when you die. In the other way, they, as well as your spouse, can also benefit. Your children will receive all of that insurance cash. By this approach, you hedge and cover your flanks.

In other words, if you opt to take 50 percent of the income to which you are entitled on retirement, and your spouse dies first, you will lose money. You would continue living on less income than you could otherwise receive. Your family, of course, would receive nothing when you die. On the other hand, if you opt for 100 percent of your retirement income (even though it will end at your death), and then purchase a term life insurance policy with 50 percent of that income, you will be no worse off than you would be, income-speaking, taking the lesser plan. You then, however, have the insurance, your spouse is protected, and your estate increases.

If your spouse should die before you, you have another choice. Since you will receive 100 percent of your retirement income, you can raise your standard of living. Cancel the term insurance policy and live on all of your income. By choosing 100 percent of your retirement income, you continue receiving that amount until you die. In this manner, you will now receive the maximum income-producing factor throughout your retirement.

It must be noted that a few companies offer excellent, very inexpensive options with their retirement plans. Notable are the New York City School System and the Du Pont retirement plans. Both have fair, reasonable, indeed most inexpensive options in the form of continued annuity-type payments for a surviving spouse, and a standard of living clause which will increase the benefits if and as the cost of living increases in the future. Unfortunately, too few companies have such fair plans.

If might well be that a retirement plan which will give you less income than 100 percent of your benefits is what you need to protect your spouse. If you are un-insurable, you must somehow protect your spouse. If he or she is ill or cannot manage money, the only practical way might be to take less than 100 percent from your retirement plan and have some form of payment continue to him or her after your death. This is an expensive road to take, but it could possibly be your only choice. Only an impartial adviser is in a position to analyze this for you. This is just one additional but important consideration before you make a retirement choice. Don't forget, the name of the game is how to get the maximum amount of income, once you retire. Why should you automatically take a minimum amount, as many of your predecessors have? You can better your situation immeasurably with valid planning before you retire.

Death benefits paid by employers to surviving family members of deceased employees are complex and might be taxable to your estate. This is another important reason why you should check before you retire and have an expert outside your company analyze all your options with you.

5

The Retirement Home

There are approximately 35,000 or more retired residents in Sun City and Youngtown, Arizona, where I practice law. There were about 700 residents when I opened my office. It is anticipated that 50,000 residents will live here by 1980. Most of them will come from other states, and foreign countries. Most people live and work with the idea that upon retirement they will move to a worry-free Shangri-la in the sunshine. There is, of course, no such place. You take your problems wherever you go, and new ones may develop.

Retirement abruptly changes one's social status. Many officers in the Armed Services, corporation executives, or active professionals earn substantial incomes while they work, where they are also in a position of authority. Once they retire, they are suddenly, and probably for the first time in many years, without authority, social status, or direction. This can be a shattering experience to the ego. Thus, in addition to the humiliation of money problems, real or imagined, there is a need to prepare for an assault on your self-image. Proper planning can minimize emotional shock and allow you to adjust gradually, gracefully, and enjoyably to your new situation.

In the community where you live and work, you are well known and liked by your friends. They respect you and will still consider you the friend, the chief, the director, the adviser. In the community where you lived and worked, you will continue to receive much of the respect you had in the past and need so desperately once you retire. If you move immediately to a new environment where you are unknown, the thrust of a changed economic position in conjunction with a new social position may be an overwhelming burden. It is the rare person, indeed, who can accept both violent changes at once. If you move immediately to your spot in the sunshine, and you are completely unknown, you will need to be a strong person to survive the emotional trauma. Do not sever your ties too abruptly or completely. The first year you retire, you might plan to spend the first few months among your family and friends. Enjoy your new freedom. Enjoy doing the things you always wanted to do. Develop interests and develop a hobby. Find some way to use your time productively.

When your first retirement winter approaches, visit your dream spot in the sunshine. Rent or lease a place for the season. Do not buy at once. If you lease, you know that you have not completely cut your ties, and you can always go home again. You will not feel insulated and isolated. You can see if you are ready for a change of environment. You can do it slowly and at your own pace. After living in a new environment six months to a year, you will know if you like it. If you do, purchase your new home and move.

At this point, recognize the importance of moving very slowly. A substantial number of new residents in retirement communities move back to their former homes. Those who no longer have cash—or will lose too much money on the resale of their "retirement" home, are often stuck. If so, they are miserable. The suicide rate is increasing in some retirement communities. It is a sad, shocking commentary on haste. This need not be. If you move slowly and graciously, you can adapt.

Retirement communities offer many advantages. However, if you drive through the sunshine states you will see isolated, badly maintained buildings by the side of the road, in the middle of nowhere. These are retirement homes in communities that were never finished. The developer was not financially secure and went bankrupt. The buyers are stuck. They cannot resell these homes. This need not be your fate. Check very carefully into the financial background of any corporation that develops a retirement community. You can do so by inquiring at the Corporation Commission's office in most states. Don't waste your savings! Be sure you purchase in a well-developed community.

You certainly will not lose your money or your investment if you consider only communities already established. It is vital that you move to a successful community. It is safer to move into an established one even if the cost is slightly higher than in a new one. Once you retire, you can't afford to lose your money!

If you rent a place for the season in a retirement community, you might consider leasing your present home. It certainly doesn't pay to leave it empty, and you would not want to sell it until you are sure you will not want to return. There might be an economic advantage in retaining your original home if you can buy a new home (in a retirement community) without the monies you would receive from the sale of your old. You could then turn your old home into an investment. You can lease the house, receive a monthly income and depreciate the house, since it now is an investment. The depreciation schedule will be such that most of the rent you receive in the form of income will be nontaxable to you for many years. You might have your financial adviser or accountant go over these facts and figures with you. This opportunity to receive tax-free income to help you in your retirement is often ignored.

Many charities are getting into the retirement business. These charities run retirement nursing homes and apartments. You purchase the right to live in such an apartment. They are quite expensive. They run between $20,000 and $40,000. You don't receive ownership or title to the apartment for this money. All you receive is an alleged lifetime use of the apartment. In addition to this fee, you will pay a monthly maintenance fee for food and the right to use all of the facil-

ities. Among the advertised facilities are "complete
medical care for the rest of your life." Some of my
clients live in such a community. After a number of
years in residence, they find that complaints are increasing. It would appear that few of these centers can truly
afford to provide the complete medical services they
advertise. There are few full-time physicians and rarely
any specialists. If you need medical treatment that requires specialization, you must provide this for yourself, and, of course, pay for it, unless you are covered
by other through insurance. Their medical facilities are
often crowded and sometimes not too comfortable. In
addition to this, some would appear to attempt to declare
their residents incompetent at the first possible opportunity. Another complaint has been that some communities move an elderly, ill, widowed person into the
infirmary and tell him he is too sick to live alone. He
must, therefore, live the rest of his days in the infirmary.
This allows the charity to immediately resell the apartment to another individual while the previous apartment-dweller is still alive. If you think that such a
retirement center is for you, you might be wise to talk
with a number of residents there and see if any of the
above-mentioned abuses are prevalent.

6

The Single Retired Person

The widow, widower, unmarried, and divorced retired person share a common problem. Many retirement communities are couple-oriented, especially designed for couples. Thus, the single person there is often lonely. In addition, as people become older, some continue to cast around for new and exciting associations. In older age, some spouses become more jealous, not less. The single retired individual is often subjected, thus, to automatic suspicion.

There are new retirement communities which provide condominium-type apartments for single individuals. You will not necessarily be lonely in such an apartment, for you will find companionship there. Choose a retirement community that provides housing for the single retired as well as couples, if you plan to move.

The information provided in this book will apply to

the single retired person, the widow, and the widower, unless you are otherwise informed in the text. Generally speaking, the decisions, the mistakes, the choices, the problems of the widow, the widower, and the single retired person will be substantially the same as those of a married couple. A married couple must, of course, plan their retirement together. The single person will do it alone. This is probably the only basic difference.

SUMMARY OF PART ONE

Plan for retirement carefully. Start at least one year before your retirement begins. Make checklists for retirement. Include the following complete and detailed analysis of your assets. All assets must have a current valid fair market value.

1. Your home and its contents.
2. Jewelry and uniquely expensive items.
3. Nonincome-producing investments, such as group ven tures in real estate.
4. Coin and stamp collections.
5. Anything else of marketable value which you own.

An additional list should detail your income potential, such as the following:

1. Social Security for you and/or your spouse.
2. Part-time work.
3. Pension and profit-sharing plans (list all choices and options).
4. All dividends from investments.
5. Rent from real estate.

6. Income from bank deposits, certificates of deposit, bonds, and the like.
7. Consultation in your field.
8. Any other source of income which you can anticipate.

A final list should include your current living expenses, such as the following:

1. Approximate budget for food.
2. Approximate cost of medicines and drugs not covered by insurance.
3. Rent.
4. Taxes (real estate, estimated income, etc.).
5. General maintenance of your home (include repairs and utilities).
6. Other expenses such as automobile maintenance, clothing, and any such related items.

When your lists are complete, analyze your financial position. This is when you look to see where you can save money. Try to eliminate all risk equities from your portfolio. You want to maintain and preserve your assets.

It is essential that you do not liquidate assets and then put your monies into a nongrowth annuity or a savings account. Such actions could mean economic disaster, if inflation continues. You must maintain the dollar value of your principal. You must maintain the purchasing power of your dollar.

Plan to live on all of your income. There is no reason for the retired to limit our enjoyment of life in an attempt to leave estates for children.

Leave your employment in the best physical condition. Complete all physical examinations while you are employed and covered by group insurance. Any future operations you can anticipate should be performed while you are covered by group insurance.

Do you really need your life insurance? Are you getting any benefits from it? Consider cashing it in and investing the cash surrender value in a conservative income producing and growth investment. This will provide additional income to you and preserve the dollar value of your assets. Many retired individuals have substantial cash surrender value in their old insurance policies. When you die you lose the cash surrender value money. Insurance policies depreciate daily. They shrink as the result of inflation. These insurance monies have less purchasing power for your heirs when you die. These policies should not be held longer than absolutely necessary. Once you retire, insurance gives you little advantage, unless you need it to pay estate taxes. Often, the reason you purchased the insurance originally is no longer a useful one.

Many people pay too much money for annual insurance premiums. If your insurance policy has a cash surrender value, this money belongs to you. A $30,000 life insurance policy that is 30 years old should have a $15,000 cash surrender value. That money is yours. With your premiums, you are purchasing only an additional $15,000' worth of insurance. However, your premiums are based on the full $30,000 policy. When you die, the company pays your heirs the $15,000 which is already yours, and only $15,000 of their own money.

This is an area of great abuse by insurance companies. If you have not already done so, it might be more prudent to take your cash surrender money now. If you need additional insurance, and I cannot imagine why you should, purchase inexpensive term insurance to cover the difference between your cash surrender value money and the additional amount you desire.

If your employer has term life insurance policies on your life as a result of your former employment, and you do not pay the premium, keep this insurance.

Find an expert and independent adviser. (This means going outside the company.) He will help you plan your retirement intelligently. Any tax-trained, estate-planning attorney is qualified to analyze your assets, do estate planning, such as wills and trusts, and analyze the various options available to you in your retirement and pension plans. Most employers do not provide an independent expert to analyze these plans to your best advantage, and many of my retired clients made the most imprudent choices.

It is often dangerous to move immediately to a new environment, where you are unknown, as soon as you retire. Do not sever your ties too abruptly or completely. Visit your dream spot in the sunshine, if you wish. Rent or lease a place for the season. Do not buy immediately. If you lease, you can always go back home without a serious financial loss. You will not be, therefore, permanently insulated and isolated. You can see if you are ready for the change of environment slowly and without risk.

If you like your new retirement home after living there six months to a year on a lease basis, it is probably safe to purchase.

Most retirement communities offer many advantages. However, some are on the verge of bankruptcy. Check into the financial background of any corporation that develops a retirement community. Be sure it is solvent, that it has assets that are not mortgaged. Don't waste your savings. It is not advisable to be the first to buy into a new retirement community. Make sure you purchase in a well-developed area. It is safer to move into an established retirement community, even if the cost is slightly higher. You cannot afford to lose your money, once you retire. If the developer does not complete his development, the home you purchased in the undeveloped, uncompleted community will be almost worthless. Above all, never buy a retirement home without visiting the community in advance.

The decisions and problems for the widow, widower, unmarried, or divorced person are substantially the same as those of a married couple. Therefore, the information in this book will apply to any single individual unless otherwise stated.

PART TWO
After You Retire

7

Educate Your Spouse

In most families, either the husband or the wife usually handles the business affairs. It is the rare family, indeed, where both husband and wife maintain the records together. Generally, either the wife maintains records, writes the family checks and pays the bills, or the husband does everything. In either case, one spouse is often completely ignorant of the family's economic facts.

When one individual handles the family assets, the other spouse is in a completely exposed position. As you approach retirement, educate your spouse. The spouse who handles the business affairs of the family must take pains to instruct the other how to write checks and keep records. Prepare a written inventory of what both of you own. Explain where everything is located, especially jewelry or anything you have in your own name.

At retirement, both spouses should begin to handle all family business affairs together. Insist that your spouse participate. Write the checks together. Analyze your problems and needs together. Make investment choices together. It certainly pays to introduce your spouse to your business adviser, broker, and other professionals who handle your affairs. Educating your spouse is the most important thing you can do for him or her when you retire. Both partners in a marriage have a duty to tell each other everything, and a right to know where all family assets are located. It is often necessary to show a wife how to maintain herself. She will then not be abused in widowhood.

Many men feel that their wives are not capable of handling business affairs. This is absurd! If she is not capable while you live, she will be less capable should you die. Start immediately if you haven't already! Educate your spouse. You abuse your entire family by indulging laziness while you live. Nothing is more pitiful than a worried widow, with no knowledge of how to cope with finances (especially if she doesn't know what she owns), in a state of shock after her husband's death. There is no greater cruelty than keeping your wife (or husband) uninformed.

Many men and women tell their children or a friend where things are, and neglect to tell a spouse. This is regrettable and silly. They usually forget, and they are the wrong ones to tell. In any event, write things down and keep a copy with your personal records, or give your lawyer a copy to keep in his file.

List in detail for each other, as the case may be, the following:

1. All separate and joint assets. Explain what these are in detail, and where they are located.

2. All of your securities, such as stocks or bonds. Tell your spouse where the certificates are located. If either of you has a street account at a broker, make sure your spouse knows the broker, the address of the office handling the account, and the account number.

3. All your insurance. Introduce your spouse to the insurance agent. If you haven't done so already, it might be advisable to write your insurance company and ask them to send you a proof-of-death claim now, so that you can keep it attached to your policy. Then your survivor will merely have to fill it out at your death. Most insurance companies don't pay interest from the time of death, so the policy should be the first thing any survivor turns in.

Also, analyze your wills both with your attorney and with each other. Make sure you both understand everything specified in the wills. Your spouse is the one who will have to live under the terms and conditions of your will, and your spouse deserves a voice in what you do.

If you live in a state that locks safety-deposit boxes at the death of the owner (and the majority of states do this), take all of your insurance papers and your will and put them into a safety-deposit box owned by your spouse, or have your attorney or other adviser hold them for you. In any event, make sure your wife or husband knows where they are and that each of you can get to the other's assets quickly.

8

Your Financial Reeducation

Don't speculate with your assets.

Now that you are retired, money problems will probably be your main concern. Your assets should be in good order, if you took the time to plan your retirement carefully. You can now no longer afford the luxury of losing money through high-risk investments, because you cannot replace your losses. You must try to protect your standard of living, and this can be done without reckless speculation in the marketplace.

There is no reason to play the market at this stage in your life. I do not mean that you should sell your good investments. I simply mean that you should stop speculating, and stop active trading. If your assets are good stocks—conservative growth stocks, conservative bonds—this is exactly what you need to hedge against inflation and preserve the buying power of your retirement monies. There is, however, no need for active trading

46

once your affairs are in good order. Before you retired, you should have converted all of your assets into conservative, high income-producing stocks or, perhaps, certain bonds. Generally speaking, conservative and preferred stocks do not fluctuate violently like most common stocks. They provide a fair and reasonable income in the way of dividends, and they occasionally split. Most important, they usually hedge against inflation over any given five-year period. Once you retire, and your affairs are in order, leave them alone. Don't worry about the market. Even when the market slumps, most dividends continue. Your income is usually not affected.

Many of your stocks may have increased in value since you purchased them. Some of these stocks are probably not the secure, income-producing and conservative kinds that you should hold, once retired. Many of my clients express a desire to change these assets, but are afraid to pay capital-gains taxes. This is silly! Most of these growth stocks pay minimum dividends. Isn't it ridiculous to sit on assets that are not producing a good income just to avoid paying capital-gains taxes? A capital-gains tax means that you have made a profit. You should not be unhappy about that. You should start to sell these nonconservative old stocks, a little at a time, and pay a modest capital-gains tax. You can then purchase a high income-producing investment, which will help you maintain your standard of living.

Buy your investments and take title (ownership) in your name alone, unless a tax-trained estate planner tells you it is safe to buy them in the name of yourself and your spouse. Joint assets can have many pitfalls, which are explained in Part Six.

Never purchase mutual funds or stocks and take title in the name of a child as joint owner with you. It is equally imprudent to purchase mutual funds in your name as trustee for someone in your family. The same is true for savings accounts. Keep your assets in your name or the names of yourself and your spouse, and you won't lose them. I don't mean to imply that all children will take their parents' assets. However, the creditors of all children will not hesitate to take their parents' assets if the children's names are on title as joint owners.

There are also investment advisers working merely to churn your investments for commissions. To justify this manipulation of your assets, some brokers attempt estate planning. Few, in fact, have any knowledge of valid estate planning. Most have no legal or tax training.

Many brokers play upon your desire to save money. They promise to save you, among other things, a probate fee. These salesmen tell you: "If you buy what I sell and take ownership [title] the way I advise, you will avoid probate." Generally speaking, you avoid probate only if you give your assets away *now*, while you live. This is preposterous! You know it. I know it. You would never buy what this salesman is offering if you actually realized what you must do to avoid probate. To avoid probate is to own nothing when you die. The only way to have nothing when you die is give it away while you live.

One ridiculous way to lose your assets is through the

use of Joint Tenancy with Right of Survivorship. Most brokers don't understand why or how probate can be delayed if title is taken in joint tenancy. They often don't care to know that this can cause gift taxes, which can greatly exceed any possible probate fee. There is also a tremendous danger that jointly-owned assets may be seized by the creditors of your joint owner.

A few brokers now realize there is a danger, but they don't necessarily know why. These brokers now push the purchase of stocks through a "trust" vehicle. This is not a living trust; this is not a real trust. This is usually worse and more dangerous, if possible, than joint tenancy. Frankly, I think it is ridiculous to use a broker for estate planning. If you do, you will probably lose money!

You would be well advised to purchase nothing from any broker who tells you that he will save you a probate fee. If he knows so little about this area, and still advises you, perhaps he has a similarly poor knowledge of the stocks he recommends.

Unfortunately, there are also some attorneys who don't understand estate taxes, or the dangers of joint property. I just read a publication, allegedly written by an attorney, which attempts to tell the reader how to avoid using a lawyer, in all applications of the law. The book states that you should avoid probate at all costs. The method suggested is joint tenancy with children. It is regrettable that there are some of my colleagues who abort their professional responsibilities by giving advice in areas of the law where they, themselves, have such limited knowledge.

Many of you will lose assets because you will follow the advice of people who are generally unqualified to discuss entitlement. Remember, the burden is on you: Get proper advice from a knowledgeable source. Recognize the limitations of many brokers or mutual-funds salesmen. Their educational background does not usually equip them to give legal advice on how you should own or take title of investments.

Don't abuse your assets!

Fear of mishandling assets causes many people to liquidate holdings upon retirement. This money is then placed into a variety of savings accounts. Banks and savings institutions enthusiastically encourage this. Again, question their motivation! It is simply profit, and the profit is not yours!

You perhaps think this is "security." It is the exact opposite. You believe all these accounts are insured, and this impresses you. Not all such accounts are 100 percent insured for you. There can be a limit of insurance that any individual can receive, regardless of the number of different joint accounts he may open in any financial institution. This includes all branch banks. Even if you are covered by insurance, why protect your money at the expense of shrinking your assets?

Savings institutions in my community have opened "Private Executive Clubs." These can only be described as a "come on" to get their hands on your money. For example, if you put $5,000 or more into a savings account at these institutions, they grant you membership privileges, such as:

1. The right to sit there all day during banking hours and read a variety of magazines.

2. The right to make one long-distance telephone call a month without charge.

3. Some alleged group-travel benefits.

4. All the free coffee (although quite weak) you can drink.

What you really receive is the most expensive cup of coffee imaginable and the most expensive telephone conversation in the history of AT&T.

Most savings and loan institutions, and most commercial banks offer a variety of savings accounts. I represented a retired top executive from a large savings institution. He was a very wealthy man. He did not have, at any time, more than $5,000 in a savings account anyplace. This should tell you something about the proper handling of money.

These institutions push their time certificates-of-deposit. This allows them to hold your money a longer period of time. You should realize these corporations are not altruistic. They are motivated by one thing: profit. They want to make money. They certainly do! A fortune is made with this money. Unfortunately, the fortune is not for the depositor.

The average savings account pays interest between 5 percent and 7 percent per annum. The average time certificate of deposit pays interest from 6 percent to 8 percent, but you must leave your money with the institution for a considerable period of time.

Inflation shrinks your money and mine today at a

distressing rate. For the month in which I am writing this chapter, hard inflation is 9½ percent. It is hoped that inflation will not continue at this high rate, but one can anticipate an approximate minimum rate of 5 percent. There is a distinct possibility it might be higher. Many economists feel that a small rate of inflation is a necessary incentive to growth. In any event, it is here to stay. It should increase yearly. Current inflation means that the buying power of your dollar shrinks at a minimum of 5 percent a year, if we can knock inflation down to that 5 percent level. If the buying power of your dollar shrinks at the rate of 5 percent a year, and you keep assets in a non-growth investment (such as a savings account), you will really earn, in actual buying power, 5 percent less than the interest they pay you. Thus, if your bank account pays 5 percent, in reality you earn zero because the buying power of your money has decreased by 5 percent in that year. You actually lost money, because your principal also depreciates in buying power. Thus, any money you placed into this financial trap is worth less every day because a savings account does not hedge against inflation.

Inflation is quite simple to understand. If you put $10,000 into one of these financial institutions in any of their interest-bearing schemes, the principal amount of $10,000 always remains at $10,000. There is no possibility of principal growth. Let's assume you receive the above, average interest of 5 percent from your bank. This produces an income of $500 a year. Assume further that you are at the minimum income tax level, and we will take only 20 percent for taxes. This leaves you the grand total of $400' worth of spendable income: only 4 percent on the $10,000. However, if the annual inflation approximates 5 percent, in reality, your $10,000 is worth less, or $9,500; therefore, you actually lost $100 each year when you received a net income of $400 after taxes, because your $10,000 today will only buy what $9,500 would have bought when you first deposited your money in that bank.

Of course, your loss is much more critical if inflation is higher. If the 9½ percent figure is reached again, you almost double your loss.

Look at it another way. Today $10,000 might allow you to buy two fully-equipped automobiles in the minimum price range. However, five years ago, these automobiles would have cost $3,500 each, or a total of $7,000. Today, five years later, it takes $10,000 to purchase the same automobiles. If you leave your money in these financial institutions for five years, it is safe to assume that five years from now, the identical automobiles will cost somewhere in the area of $6,500 to $7,000 each. Your $10,000, therefore, will no longer buy you two minimum-price cars. Perhaps, it will buy you one minimum-price car and a tricycle. You might, however, be lucky enough to purchase two compacts. The same principle applies in the purchase of bread and wine. Inflation depreciates the value of your dollar day by day, year after year. You must, therefore, put your assets into a secure investment that pays fair dividends and still allows your principal to increase conservatively and slowly, but enough to hedge against inflation. Fixed investments do not! Life insurance does not! Annuities do not! Many bonds do not! Savings accounts do not!

One must be quite wealthy to afford the luxury of investments that do not increase the principal value. That is why I repeat throughout this book that you must insure maximum income and see to it that both income and principal retain their buying power. In other words, you must hedge against inflation. This is another reason to seriously consider the purchase of safe, secure, income-producing investments, or certain bonds that can pay sufficient income and hedge against inflation over any given five year period of time, by increasing in market value enough to offset the rise in the cost of living through inflation.

It goes without saying that I do not believe any retired person should purchase tax-free bonds unless he has an income in excess of $20,000. The average retired individual is not at an income tax level that justifies the loss of all growth potential with the purchase of these bonds.

Why is it important to hedge against inflation? Clearly, if you take all your retirement assets and convert them into cash, you will never be worth any more than you presently are. If the value of the dollar shrinks, which means that the cost of things will increase, your standard of living must, therefore, decrease every year.

You might think that the security of insured bank accounts is worthwhile. However, $50,000 in a savings institution in five years will probably be worth only $40,000 in real buying power. This becomes critical when you consider the cost of food. Even beer will be too expensive for you as inflation slowly, constantly, minimizes the real buying power you have. Five years from now, with your principal thus invested, you will be unable to maintain your present standard of living.

It is undeniably prudent to have some cash savings for emergencies. It is, however, absurd to place all of your assets into a financial institution which offers nothing but a trap. The advertisements tell you about daily interest; they don't mention the daily shrinkage of your principal. You must realize that both exist!

Remember, once again, that the name of the game is how to enjoy the maximum income during your retirement, consistent with maximum security. This assumes there will be a reasonable conservative growth in the real value of your assets, in order to hedge against inflation and preserve the buying power of your money.

The average retired person arrives at his Shangri-la with a pocketful of cash. Many financial institutions conduct active, aggressive campaigns to get their hands on this money. They are quite creative.

The ways that some savings institutions actively attack you are manifestly preposterous and morally outrageous. They bombard you in attempts to grab all of your money. Then they pay you what amounts to approximately 1 to 2 percent income in real buying power, after the shrinkage from inflation and income tax is deducted. All the free coffee in the world hardly makes this abuse worthwhile.

If you are enamored of your favorite financial institution, you would be better off to buy its stock. You will be ahead of your neighbor, who simply puts all of his money into the institution's savings plans.

Check the insurance company that insures your savings bank (and your accounts) very carefully. Be sure it has assets of value behind it. Most banks and savings institutions are insured. Not all financial institutions have Federal Deposit Insurance Corporation protection or Federal Savings and Loan Insurance Corporation protection. There are some financial institutions which insure themselves with private insurance companies. This fact should give you pause! Why can't they insure with the appropriate federal insurance corporation? Is it perhaps because they cannot qualify for this insurance? Are they doing something wrong? It's bad enough that these institutions guarantee a loss in buying power, without risking the loss of all your money at once.

Sometimes the corporations which insure bank accounts and savings accounts are owned by the stockholders or directors of the very same bank or savings institution. In many communities anyone can buy an old insurance charter not presently in use. In these communities a bond as low as $250,000, filed with the Insurance Commission, is all that is necessary to form a valid insurance company. It's possible that some companies have few assets beyond that $250,000 cash bond.

There are some financial institutions with millions

of dollars in savings accounts, insured only by this $250,000 cash bond. It is a grotesque situation! It is even more grotesque because the insurance commissioners do nothing to correct these abuses. Once you have lost your money, it does you no good to question whether these insurance commissioners exist to protect you, or to protect the insurance companies. *You* must protect *yourself*, and investigate in advance.

If that savings institution which is insured by an insurance company with nothing but that $250,000 cash bond goes broke, only the first $250,000' worth of claims will be protected and paid. You have a duty to yourself, therefore, to be sure that the insurance company which insures your account is a company with sufficient assets. You are retired. You have the time. Check around. Protect yourself! Be careful!

Remember, too, that any investment and any savings institution which offers you interest well above the average may be carrying a risk factor. It is not wise for you to assume any unnecessary risks once you retire.

Even financial institutions with the appropriate federal insurance can only insure one individual's account in that bank up to $40,000. In order to grab more of your money, these institutions invented a variety of ways for you to open different accounts. Most of these peculiar accounts may place you in severe financial danger.

In my state, some salespeople who open new accounts for the banks and savings institutions urge you to always open the account in your name, with your spouse as joint tenant. They further urge you to open an account with your child's name on the account. In addition, they urge you to open another account with you and your spouse each acting as trustee for the other. They also advise additional accounts, wherein you act as trustee for your children! And so it goes. Unfortunately, very few of these salespeople understand the legal complications of entitlement.

As a reasonably intelligent person, if you were told repeatedly by experts that something you were doing was wrong or immoral, would it not give you pause? If you were also informed that there are serious dangers in what you are doing, wouldn't you also ask, "Why?" If you were a salesman and were told that the advice you were giving those who use your services was not only incorrect but also dangerous, wouldn't you attempt to learn more?

Oddly enough, those salespeople who are hired to sell different savings accounts do not care to thus educate themselves. They are generally more interested in winning a free weekend at a resort, for selling a certain number of savings accounts in any given monthly period.

For some reason, the financial institutions do not, themselves, train their sales staffs to understand the legal significance of the accounts they promote. My colleagues and I have pleaded with sales personnel at banks and savings institutions not to recklessly advise the use of joint tenancy. We further call attention to the danger when a bank account is opened in your name as trustee

for another person. Nevertheless, these financial institutions want your money so desperately that they ignore
the dangers and allow members of their staffs to practice
law without a license—and, most important, without the
proper education. You suffer the consequences. The
standard response of these salespeople is, "We don't
agree with the attorneys." I can only assume that these
same individuals, if told by their physicians that they
needed medicine, would say, "We don't agree with
you."

Their rationale seems to be that joint tenancy elimi-
nates probate. It does not—it merely delays probate. Tax
consequences can actually cost more than probate; you
can also lose these accounts to the creditors of your
joint owner.

Now that you know the limitations of educational
background, legal knowledge, and understanding of
these bank clerk-salesmen, perhaps you will not rely too
heavily on their advice.

Once you are aware that the primary motivation of
banks and savings institutions is to get your money,
perhaps you will be more cautious. Let us not blame
the banks or the bank clerks or the savings institutions
for our own errors. It is human nature to wish to appear
more knowledgeable than we are. Everyone likes to give
advice. However, you wouldn't go over to a sales clerk
at a department store and ask his advice as to what you
should do in a major real estate transaction. You
wouldn't ask this person what to do with any of your
assets, would you? Why, therefore, would you ask a

mere clerk-salesman at a savings institution what to do with your assets? He doesn't understand the complexities of entitlement or ownership of assets. Once again, the burden to protect yourself is on you.

Should you ask an officer in any of these institutions the questions you ask the clerk-salesman, the officer would probably tell you he is not authorized to practice law. He would suggest you visit an attorney. Banks and savings institutions are in great error for not instructing clerks to do the same thing.

When I question these clerks, they say to me, "We don't advise customers. People insist that everything be put in joint tenancy." When I question my clients, they say, "The tellers at the bank get angry if we don't take their advice. They demand that we make everything joint or in trust." One thing is sure; you no longer have reason to make this mistake. You now realize that these clerks are not experts, and if you follow their advice, you do so at your own peril!

In later chapters concerning trusts and joint tenancy, I will explain some of the dangers in more detail. For now, please be aware that you should never have a savings or checking account of any type in anyone's name but your own, if you are a single person. If you are married, and it is a *first* marriage and only a *first* marriage, it *might* be safe to consider using a joint tenancy account. You should never use a joint tenancy account with a second spouse unless you enjoy risking the possibility that you will disinherit your children. This is explained in detail in Part Six. Joint tenancy can be expensive. It can be expensive even with a husband or wife if your total assets exceed $100,000, for you might have to pay excessive estate taxes at death. Never, *absolutely never*, put a child's name on anything you own. This is particularly true of bank accounts, stocks, and your home. Should you do this, you might suffer severe gift taxes which greatly exceed any savings on a probate —and worse, you can lose these assets to the creditors of your joint owner.

The primary reason that some financial institutions recommend these various accounts is because they want to get their hands on all of your money. They realize you want an insured account, and each account cannot be insured beyond a limited amount. Therefore, they recommend these questionable methods of holding your assets. Usually, they tell you that all of these different savings accounts which you own are insured. Often, these accounts are not fully insured to you. Let me repeat, for this is important. If you had your name on different savings accounts with different people, while these accounts might be insured under certain circumstances, there is not 100 percent insurance in each instance to both of the joint owners. You are only entitled to a limited amount of insurance from joint accounts. In other words, joint accounts can split your insurance. For example, assume you placed your daughter's name on your $20,000 savings account. The account now reads "You and your daughter as joint tenants with right of survivorship." The bank subsequently goes broke. (Banks still do this.) In this example, assume the insurance was government insurance, so it will ultimately be paid. It might take one to two years to receive your money. Before the insurance is paid there must be a complete audit of all accounts in that bank and all bank assets. This is yet another reason why you should not have more than one savings account at any one financial institution, even if there is full insurance. Why not spread your risk so that if the financial institution goes broke, you won't tie up all of your assets. If you insist upon multiple savings accounts, at least use different banks for each account. In any event, whenever the above account is paid off by the insurance company, you will receive only $10,000. Your daughter will receive the other $10,000. Now I know *your* daughter will give you back that $10,000, but your neighbor's daughter might not—especially since she will be making her parent a gift of the $10,000, on which she might well have to pay gift taxes.

Most financial institutions know insurance monies can be split, yet they give the impression that these additional accounts are fully insured to you. A reasonable person might ask why these financial institutions suggest such accounts. I have never received a direct answer from any financial institution I've questioned. The obvious reason is profit. This is fine for the bank. But you, unfortunately, don't share the profit, and you accept all the risks. Until you read the information on trusts and joint tenancy, be aware! Remember: It is dangerous, and it can be very expensive to use joint tenancy on any bank account, unless you are husband and wife in a first marriage and your total assets are less than $100,000. Never, absolutely never, put a bank account in your name as trustee for someone else! This can be financial suicide. Never put a child's name on any of your assets! If you do any of these things, there is a chance that you will lose them.

It is essential to have a savings account. We must prepare for emergencies. There is, however, a substantial difference between having an emergency savings account and placing all of your assets into a variety of savings accounts. These accounts can cause you to lose your money, and, if nothing else, lessen the buying power of your money through inflation.

I am an enthusiastic believer in reasonable savings accounts. I also believe you should not abuse your assets by putting everything you own into them.

SUMMARY OF PART TWO

There is nothing more cruel that you can do to your spouse than to keep him or her uninformed. It is your mutual duty to demand that you both know everything. It is essential that both of you learn how to maintain family records, pay bills, handle investments, and write checks together. Both of you must know your assets, which means both your joint assets and the things you might own in your own names alone. Each one of you must know the location of everything and the names of

your advisers; it is the duty of all spouses to educate
each other. Do not leave your spouse in the dark.

Once you retire, stop speculating with your assets.
This does not mean you should take good assets out of
the marketplace and waste them in savings accounts.

If the stocks you own are not income-producing
stocks, but have greatly increased in value through the
years, do not hesitate to sell them. Too many retired
people don't sell nonincome-producing investments
simply because they do not wish to pay a capital-gains
tax. A capital-gains tax means profit. It is shortsighted
not to be willing to pay this tax when you can do so
and then purchase an income-producing investment.
Remember, you must constantly try to obtain the maximum income with maximum security when you retire.
It is absurd to hold back valuable assets, which could
otherwise be producing income for you. When you
purchase assets after retirement, put them in your name
alone, or in your name and your spouse's name if a tax-
trained adviser tells you that is prudent. Above all,
never put your child's name on anything you own.
Should you do this, there is a high probability that you
will lose it while you live.

Don't liquidate all of your assets and put them into
savings accounts. It is important and necessary to keep
an emergency savings account. Any fully insured savings institution with insurance carried by one of the
federal agencies is a good place for this emergency account. It is imprudent, however, to have more than one
savings account, or more than $10,000 in cash wasting

away in a savings institution. Time certificates of deposit and savings accounts depreciate daily as a result of inflation. They lose money for you every single day. Their buying power decreases every day. If you take all of your assets and put them into savings institutions, your income in five years might not allow you to eat properly. In five years, inflation should take a good 25 percent of the value of your money. Only have *one* emergency savings account, and put the rest of your assets into a secure, conservative, income-producing investment that will protect you and hedge against inflation.

PART THREE
Wills

9

Your Probate Lawyer and Your Executor

A will is never probated! Let me repeat, a will is *never* probated! An estate is probated with or without a will. A will makes the probate less expensive. Generally, it completes the process of passing your assets on to your heirs quickly and efficiently, with minimum costs.

Simply put, your will is your declaration of intent. It is a statement of what you want done with your assets after your death. Anyone who owns anything of value or will inherit something of value should have a will. This is especially true of a husband and wife who always inherit from each other.

Just think: You spent your time and fortune gathering your assets throughout your lifetime. You always sought the best advice. Now, you plan to give these assets away, often without expert advice. Or, you plan to dispose of everything in a five-minute conference with a lawyer. You give no proper thought either to what you have or to what you really wish done with it. You are transferring the total assets of your life. They certainly deserve some serious consideration. There are many possibilities, many alternatives.

The probate lawyer is an expert in the field of estate planning, which includes the drafting of legal documents, such as wills and trusts. He is the logical person to give you advice.

Of course, not making a will at all is the ultimate irresponsibility, but nothing is more subject to expensive court fights, wasted taxes, and abuse of your assets than those mistakes made in avoiding probate. It is difficult to understand the current tendency to accept, as fact, the elaborate nonsense written about this subject, without considering either the author's qualifications or his money-making motives. All too often, life insurance companies present you with pamphlets proclaiming that they can do your estate planning for you—and without charge! They are trying to sell you insurance. This is O.K., so long as you understand their motivation. Usually, they are not actually interested in minimizing your taxes or true estate planning. The stockbroker who tells you how to take title (ownership), and the real estate broker who tells you he can handle your deeds, or that you don't need a will if you take title in joint tenancy, are misleading you.

All states acknowledge and allow one particular type of will. This is the formal will. It is prepared by your attorney after he interviews you and ascertains what you want. He will also advise you on the most efficient way both to minimize estate and inheritance taxes, and to distribute assets to your heirs. The most well-advised among you already have such a will.

Another type of will, which is also a written will, is called a holographic will. This is a will written entirely in the handwriting of the deceased. Seventeen states and Puerto Rico allow you to use such a will without any limitations.* Twenty-three states and the District of Columbia do not allow such a will.† The remaining states and territories allow such a will under certain specific, unique circumstances. Some of them require that a holographic will be witnessed. Others require that you be out of the United States for one year, or in military service and away from home for one year, and the requirements or forms that apply vary.

A holographic will is at best a tricky and expensive procedure. You would be well advised never to use one. This is particularly true if you live in a state that allows it but only under certain conditions. You had better know these conditions. It is safe to assume that you should not use a holographic will.

Should you be ambitious enough to write your own will, be sure that it is written entirely in your own

---

* Alaska, Arizona, Arkansas, California, Idaho, Louisiana, Mississippi, Montana, Nevada, Oklahoma, Pennsylvania, Puerto Rico, South Dakota, Tennessee, Texas, Utah, Virginia, West Virginia.

† Alabama, Colorado, Connecticut, Delaware, District of Columbia, Florida, Georgia, Hawaii, Illinois, Indiana, Kansas, Kentucky, Maine, Massachusetts, Michigan, Minnesota, Missouri, Nebraska, New Hampshire, New Mexico, Ohio, Oregon, South Carolina, Wyoming.

handwriting. Date the will above your signature and sign it on the bottom. Make certain nobody else writes anything on the paper. Be sure you do not type or print such a will. It must be written entirely in your hand, to be valid in most states. This will should not be witnessed by anyone, unless the state requires witnesses. The fact that it is written entirely in your handwriting will be enough, once your signature and handwriting is established and proven. In those states that require the holographic will to be written entirely in your handwriting, and without witnesses, anyone else's signature on the will voids it.

My state (Arizona), through its new statute, allows a holographic will to be partially written and partially typed or printed. Those portions which must be in handwriting are the "material" parts of the will. The draftors of this unique statute, and the legislators who passed it, neglected to define a "material" provision.

The privilege of making a will stems from the Statute of Wills enacted in England in 1540. Before that time, various property rights escheated to the state, or specifically to the crown, when the owner died. From 1540 on, various landholders, in return for their services to the King, were allowed to distribute their property first to their eldest male child. After many centuries and family feuds, manipulations, developments, and laws, both in England and the U.S., today every state has a statute listing the requirements concerning a will. Since this privilege is granted to you, and it is not a right (such as the right of free speech under the Constitution), you must meet the requirements of your particular state statute. If you do not know or cannot understand exactly what that statute says, then it is ridiculous to prepare your own will.

You do not necessarily save money by writing your own will! Generally, you are apt to make expensive errors. As an estate lawyer, I have seen and, indeed, probated many holographic wills. Every one of these wills cost more to probate than a formal will prepared by a competent attorney would have cost. This is a very technical area, and it does not usually make sense to save the very few dollars any competent lawyer would charge for the preparation of a formal will.

Anyone above the age of 18 can prepare a will, or have a will prepared. The person making the will must have what is known as "testamentary capacity." In other words, he must have the legal knowledge to make a will. In most states, this means three things:

1. Know what you are doing (making a will).

2. Know what you own (your assets).

3. Know who the law considers to be the natural objects of your property. This usually means spouse, your children, your mother, or your father. In other words, you must know your exact legal relationship to those relatives (step-, foster and otherwise) who are one generation before and after you.

The fact that you must have testamentary capacity to make a will does not mean that you must leave your assets to any of these individuals. With the exception of one state (Louisiana), all states and possessions which comprise the United States allow you the privilege to do whatever you want with your assets. Louisiana alone follows the Napoleonic Code, and has what is referred to as "forced heirship," whereby some assets must be left to one's children. The Napoleonic Code, which comes from France, is substantially different from Common Law, which comes from England. You will be well advised to visit an attorney in the jurisdiction where you live, if you wish to have a proper will made. There are pitfalls everywhere.

Once you prove that you have testamentary capacity, that there is no undue influence (that nobody, in other words, is twisting your arm or forcing you to make the will), and that you are of sound mind, then you can do whatever you wish, and leave your assets to whomever you choose.

You can do almost anything you want with a will. Some people use a will during their lifetimes to control their heirs. Others use a will to dispose of not only their assets, but also their ill feelings.

Once I had a client who wanted his will to read:

To my former son-in-law, the miserable so-and-so, whom I supported all these years, and who had the complete lack of taste to leave my daughter for that tramp with whom he now lives, heartburn! Heartburn which he should have forever and which I leave him in abundance.

Now, this is dangerous! It is also silly. You really should not libel anyone under your will. You may well ask, "Why not?" One clever individual said, "Let them exhume me and sue me." "They" don't have to. "They" can sue your estate. "They" can sue your executor. An estate and an executor can be liable for the torts of the deceased. So try to avoid being nasty in your will!

One person demanded that I put the following clause into his will. I did it because he insisted, and I did not consider it libelous. The paragraph read:

I leave the sum of $2,000 in trust, for one (1) year [naming a trustee], to be used for a marker for my former son-in-law's grave. Should good fortune dictate that he use it within a year of my death, fine; otherwise this Trust shall terminate, and the assets shall revert to my estate.

It's best to avoid such passions in a will. Just be aware that you should use a will merely to give your property away, not to insult or libel anyone.

Once you decide whom you wish to remember in your will, and approximately in what manner, seriously consider using percentages. For example, if you say, "To my favorite child [or niece, or anyone], Martha, $10,000, and everything else to be divided equally among the rest of my children," you might well have specific amounts in mind for the other heirs. Ten thousand dollars might represent a modest portion of your estate. It might be a large percentage. In any event, if misfortune befalls you and you must spend or lose many of your assets, $10,000 might be an exceptionally large portion of your estate. You might not want such an overwhelmingly large slice of your assets to go to one person. If your estate greatly increases, it would, of course, work the other way. Perhaps you would want Martha to receive more. It would be more prudent of you to say to yourself: "This figure represents ten percent, or twenty percent, or whatever of my estate. Therefore, I will give Martha that percentage, rather than $10,000." This percentage will now always remain constant, no matter what happens to your assets. The percentage that Martha will receive, in relationship to the other heirs, will always be the same. It is, therefore, much easier to use percentages, when you divide up your assets. It will also be easier, thus, to handle the administration of your estate. A more easily handled estate certainly means fewer expenses.

It is possible, and worthwhile, to consider listing specific legacies in your will. A specific bequest is a gift of a particular thing. It is always personal property that has an intrinsic value, such as a family Bible or personal jewelry—things that you want a particular individual to have.

During my career, I have drawn in excess of 3,000 wills. Almost every client for whom I have drawn a will has begun by saying something like this: "Oh, yes, my family understands that my daughter is to receive my jewelry and the family Bible, and my son is to receive the mahogany bed that has been in the family for many centuries."

The family might understand this, but unless you state it explicitly in your will, your executor will be obliged to do only what your will says. Otherwise, a particular heir might not receive his specific legacy—unless he or she buys it.

List all such specific legacies, in detail, in your will. Prepare a list before visiting your lawyer, so that he can incorporate it into the will. It should include your jewelry, any items of unique value, family heirlooms— possessions on which value of any kind can be placed. Thus, you save your family from misunderstandings which may well leave ill feeling after you are gone. Above all, don't leave all your personal assets to one person to distribute among your relatives. It is cruel to put such a burden on any one member of your family. It is your duty to do this yourself. Don't feel that your own children are unique. Daily, clients tell me, "My children will not fight." This is lovely. It is a great, ennobling thought. But if your children are not fighting, and my children are not fighting, who is doing all the fighting?

Never leave cash assets to one individual to distribute to the rest of the family. If one person inherits your money under a will, and the will itself does not expressly state that your money is to be divided (in whatever proportions) among other individuals, this person owns the money. This person has no legal duty to do anything but keep the money. From my own experience, the child who inherits all the money usually keeps it. Even if you leave all of your money to one child because you know for certain that he or she will split it up as you wish among your other children, you almost inevitably cause bad family feelings. Furthermore, you force this one person to waste his or her exemptions and exclusions from gift taxes. In other words, if that one child owns all of your money because you willed it to him, and that child then gives it to your other children without any *legal* duty to do this, he will be making gifts. Whenever anyone makes a gift, the party who makes the gift must pay gift taxes, if the gift exceeds $3,000 to one person in one year, and if he or she has used up his or her lifetime exemptions. Gift taxes are very tricky. The layman should not make gifts without expert advice.

You must remember here that you cannot put the burden on one person, child or friend, to distribute your assets. Not only is it unfair, but if that individual drops dead one hour after you, those assets then belong to that person's estate. They will pass to that person's family or children or whomever that person said should receive his estate under his will. You would have, thereby, disinherited your other intended heirs. Don't do such a foolish thing! If you want your assets to be distributed among different individuals, say so explicitly in your will. There can then be no misunderstandings.

Once you have distributed all of your assets in your will, you must then name an executor. This person, or institution, then has the legal duty to administer your estate. If you don't name an executor in your will, the Court will appoint an administrator. The difference between an administrator and an executor is money. An administrator *always* costs more.

An executor simply follows the directions in your will. An executor can be excused, in most instances, from posting bond. You must expressly excuse the bond in your will; otherwise the law requires that an executor post such a bond. An administrator cannot be excused. An administrator must follow the law, regardless of what you say in your will, and he must post that bond. Estate bonds cost 1 percent of the estate per year. What an elaborate waste of money!

One reason I am not anxious to recommend that any client use a human being as an executor is that human beings become ill, or they can refuse to serve. They can become involved in their own affairs, and estates can drag on. Thus, administrators must be appointed by the court to correct the errors of your now unavailable human executor. Bonds must then be filed, and so it goes. The disposal of your estate becomes expensive.

It is unfortunate and misleading to blame an efficient probate system for *your* errors in naming executors. Human beings are mortal. They die. They suffer the frailties of all mortals. In most cases, if you check carefully into an estate that has allegedly been dragging through court, and which allegedly costs an unreasonable amount of money to probate, you will find that it was handled by an individual who had no knowledge of what he or she was doing. If you are imprudent enough to name an incompetent executor—one without education, without experience, without background, without the ability to do the job—why blame the legal system for your own errors? While you live, would you allow this same person to invest your money, or tell you what to do with your assets? Of course not! Why, then, would you let this person handle your estate?

It would be prudent to seriously consider naming a financial institution as your executor. The full-service bank in your community usually has a good, competent Trust Department. The people there are experts. They are efficient, qualified executors. They charge no more than an incompetent nephew would eventually cost. Any executor is usually paid by an award from the court. These awards are not great. In my community, it is 4 percent for the first $100,000 and 2 percent thereafter. This is not a large sum to pay for efficiency. A relative will receive the same award from the court, and in addition he will have to hire accountants, advisers, assistants, real estate brokers, and the like, greatly increasing the cost of probating any estate. The full-service bank Trust Department, as executor, offers all of these services, without extra charge, for the one fee.

The Trust Department in a full-service bank is where the experts are to be found. They have the facility, the knowledge, the background, the real estate expertise, and their accountants to do the job correctly. They also have individuals with sufficient business background to preserve and maintain your business, if you should leave one. They can even sell the business as a valid asset; an incompetent executor can destroy it.

It can also be expensive to name an inexperienced relative, just because you feel that a relative should handle your affairs. If you would not go to this relative for investment advice, legal services, or tax problems, why should you turn to him to execute your will once you are dead?

Seriously consider the dangers when you name just anyone as an executor. It usually costs more money. Name a financial institution, and the job will be done quickly, efficiently, with a minimum expense.

Clients often ask me: "How much money does the state take from my estate?" No money is automatically paid to the state. Your assets would only escheat to the state today if your entire family line were wiped out and you leave no will. There would be, therefore, no living children, grandchildren, or other relatives—parents, grandparents, sisters, brothers, nieces, sideways, ad infinitum, forever. Somehow a relative always manages to "come out of the closet," in situations like this. If you have a living relative, your assets will never go to the state.

I am constantly asked: "Why do I need a will? Can I not use joint tenancy?" These questions will be answered in Part Six, but for now, be aware that joint tenancy can never replace a will. Everyone should have a will!

The signing of a will is a most serious act. All states recommend a specific method of signing called "Execution." Generally speaking, two or three witnesses are necessary. The witnesses should watch you sign the will, although they need not read it. In fact, it is not wise to let them read it. Your lawyer will most likely tell you to simply state, "This is my will."

Once you sign the will in front of all witnesses, the witnesses are asked to sign the will in each other's presence and in your presence. This isn't always necessary, but in some states each must sign in front of everyone else. Do this in order to play safe and make sure your will is valid in every state.

Contested wills are very expensive. Should you improperly execute (sign) your will, once again, the legal system cannot be blamed for a tremendous loss of assets. You would be well advised, having read this far, to recognize that a will should only be prepared by an expert and executed (signed) under his directions.

Finally, once you have your completed will, where should you keep it? A will should not be placed in a safety-deposit box. Most states require all safety-deposit boxes to be locked immediately upon your death. The box cannot be opened until there are state and federal audits. This takes a substantial amount of time. Your will should be held by your executor. If you name a bank as executor, the bank usually holds the original will without charge, in their Trust Department vaults. This is the safest and most efficient way to protect your will. Should you insist upon naming a relative as executor, then let him retain your original will in his safety-deposit box.

As a final thought, some states might consider your will revoked if you write on the original, formal will after it has been signed. Should you wish to make notes, because you want to change your will or for any other related reason, use a copy. Do *not* mark over an original will. In many states, this automatically revokes the will.

Many good estate planners feel you should never use a friend or relative to write your will. That person might have a vested interest in who gets what. This is particularly true if you use your in-laws' lawyer. In any event, there are certain basic truths about wills that apply to everyone. They are:

1. Insurance salesmen, bank employees, mutual funds salesmen, and stock brokers are not estate planners. They are commission salesmen. They do not know how to plan estates or draft wills. They don't work for nothing. You will pay them—only you don't know it. You wouldn't believe how expensive they really are.

2. Everyone who reads this book should have a will. Certainly every husband and wife has a duty to protect each other and their children.

3. There are no do-it-yourself kits for wills. Home-made wills always cost more money to probate.

4. Your will should be written so that, if you die tomorrow, what you want to happen will happen. If your wishes should later change, redo your will. A will might not be good forever. If conditions change, so must your will. You see a doctor, dentist, and accountant more than once. Perhaps you should check your will at least every five years, if not more often.

5. Do not copy your old will, trying to change it all by yourself. You will make expensive and critical mistakes. Every time two Congressmen or two legislators meet for lunch, they change some law. There is no way for you to know if the requirements to do what you want done have changed. The old patent-medicine man is gone, but the 25¢ will form survives at every stationery store. Don't use one. Do not copy your neighbor's

will. You do not wear the same size shoes or clothing as your neighbor and you certainly will have different assets, taxes, and possessions to give away. Your family might have different requirements. A will should fit you like a made-to-order suit. No two people have the exact same situation. Have your lawyer make your will to fit your needs and wishes and tax requirements. Much of the alleged probate loss will be eliminated if you have your lawyer make a will that fits you.

6. Not every lawyer is qualified to do complicated tax-estate planning. If he is not a tax-trained specialist, he probably has a colleague who is. Ask him to introduce you.

7. Be honest with your lawyer. He cannot draft a proper will for you if you lie to him. Lawyers usually charge on the basis of what they do and the time it takes. If your lawyer is not aware of your assets, he cannot save you tax money. You might end up with a simple will that could be very expensive to execute once you die. You are not a simple person, and you might need more than a simple will. Take the time to plan your will carefully.

8. If you have a second marriage, be sure and redo your will after the second marriage. If you don't, terrible things can happen.

9. Do not plan your will without your spouse being present throughout the entire process. Each husband and wife must make their needs and wishes known. Each has a right to know what the other is doing. Each has a duty to say if he can or cannot live with what the

other is doing. Remember: Your beneficiaries must live by what that will says. How would you like to live under these conditions you may be imposing on your spouse?

10

What Happens If You Die Without a Will?

In the time of the Common Law, the only individuals who could inherit from each other were heirs of the blood. This meant children, parents, brothers, and sisters. If a husband died without a will, he disinherited his wife. If a wife died without a will, she, of course, disinherited her husband. This was very harsh, and state legislatures passed laws to minimize this hardship. They did a rather bad job, and, in most states if you die without a will, your spouse still gets very poor treatment.

State legislatures passed laws which are entitled "Descent and Distribution or Succession." These statutes direct what happens if you die without a will. Some states allow up to 50 percent of your assets to pass to a spouse, and the other 50 percent to be divided among your children. Other states give your spouse only one-third of your property. Still other states give your spouse only one-third of your personal property and a lifetime use in less than all of your real estate. You might, therefore, find yourself living in a home that is truly owned by a daughter-in-law whom you dislike, if your husband died without a will. This is a ridiculous situation! Insist that your spouse adequately protect you and draw a proper will.

As an example, if a spouse dies without a will in my state, the following disaster takes place, under our new probate code. All separate property and half of the community property belonging to the deceased spouse passes to the surviving spouse. If there is no surviving spouse, but there are surviving children who are also the children of the deceased spouse, everything goes to the children in equal shares.

If there is a surviving spouse, but there are also children surviving the deceased as a result of another marriage, the children of the former marriage will get half of the deceased's separate property and no interest in the community property.

We then have a section in our statute which is entitled, "Shares of Heirs Other Than Surviving Spouse." Under this statute, if someone dies without a will, and there is no surviving spouse, everything will go equally to the children of the deceased. Our statute also says that when there is no will, "children" mean adopted children and children born out of wedlock. It doesn't say that children must have been acknowledged during the lifetime of the deceased. This is an invitation for many people to claim they are children born out of wedlock, whenever a rich person dies without a will. This shows you the absurdity of some of the statutes that some state legislatures pass. In my state, if the deceased has no living children, his assets go to grandchildren, if any. This often generates the need for guardianships to be established for grandchildren who are minors, since minors cannot handle their own affairs. Such guardianships are also very expensive.

None of my 3,000-plus clients whose wills I prepared were aware of any danger. Nevertheless, our statute is a typical example of the equally bad statutes in all states. If you die without a will, weird things can happen to your property.

Our statute goes on and says what happens if someone dies and has no surviving wife, husband, parent, brothers or sisters. What it generally means is that cousins and other relatives that you don't know probably inherit your assets.

It is necessary that you recognize the danger of not protecting your own affairs. You must obtain your own independent counsel to interpret your state statutes for you, so that you can understand what must be done, and how you must protect yourself and your family.

What all such statutes mean, however, is that your property does not escheat to the state anymore. Every state has a different law to determine what happens if you die without a will. The percentages are different, but they are all bad. To die without a will leaves a complicated mess, which is expensive to straighten out. It is ridiculous, therefore, not to prepare one.

In Arizona we have the added complication of community property.* There are 8 states and Puerto Rico that follow the laws of community property. The laws of community-property jurisdictions in each of these cases are different. Do not attempt to analyze them yourself. You must have the advice of an expert. Just be aware that, for many reasons, it is a foolish and dangerous thing to die without a will. All states have some type of law protecting a spouse. The percentages are different, but the results are always the same—bad!

Some states allow a spouse to ignore the will and take a percentage against the estate regardless of what was specified in the will. These percentages vary from 33⅓ to 50 percent. Should you write a will and give your spouse less than she or he could otherwise receive by waiving your will, you invite an expensive lawsuit. Such an act is also guaranteed to cause difficulty among your relatives. This is just another reason for a properly drafted, *formal* will, prepared with valid legal advice.

---

* Community property is those assets which someone earns while married and living in a community property state. The important words are "earns," "married," and "residing in a community-property state." Your assets don't become community property if you retire and move to a community-property state later in life.

11

Your Old Will

Clients constantly ask if an old will, drawn in another state, is "good" in Arizona. I tell them it is valid, but I doubt that it is good. Any will prepared by an attorney and properly executed (signed) often can be valid in any other state, if it does not violate some basic law in the state of current residence. However, this does not make it a "good" will. Generally speaking, any will drawn in one state is not good or easy to use in another.

You mean more than "good" when you ask that question. What you probably intend to ask is, "Can that old will, drawn in another state, be used efficiently, inexpensively, and get the job done?" Most assuredly it cannot!

Your old will declares that you are a resident of your old state. You might be subjecting your estate to dual residency and possible double taxes. In addition, the witnesses to your old will live in your former state. It is

90

difficult, expensive, and time-consuming to obtain the testimony of these out-of-state witnesses. Witnesses are necessary; they are used to prove that you had testamentary capacity, and that there was no undue influence which forced you to make the will against your wishes. Generally, if a witness is alive, he must testify at the probate hearing before your will can be admitted to probate. What an enormous expense! What an elaborate waste of time and money! The delay and cost to your estate must greatly exceed any legal fee to prepare a new will in a state where you now reside.

There are other reasons not to rely on that old will. As we have noted, you have no basic *right* to make a will. It is a privilege granted to you by each state. The laws in each state are different. The requirements are also different. Your old attorney cannot be expected to know the laws in every other state. Your old will might be subject to attack on many grounds. Why take such a foolish chance? When you move to a new state, always prepare a new will.

SUMMARY OF PART THREE

Nothing replaces a will! Life insurance does not replace a will. Joint tenancy with right of survivorship does not replace a will. A will is never probated. An *estate* is probated, with or without a will. The will simply makes it cheaper. You save money for your family with a proper will. And you make sure your wishes are followed.

Don't attempt to write your own will! This is a technical task, and you are bound to make mistakes. You are giving away the accumulations of your lifetime. Spend some time and give it serious thought. Obtain the advice of a competent estate planner. In order to write a will, a person should have an understanding and knowledge of gift taxes, estate taxes, inheritance taxes, income taxes, and the laws of the state where you reside. If you don't have this specialized knowledge, don't write your own will. If your adviser does not have this knowledge, don't let him write your will. Employ the services of an estate-planning attorney. He will save money for you, for your estate, and for your children or heirs.

It is always expensive to name a layman without experience as your executor. If you would not let this person direct your market investments, your real estate investments, or control your bank account while you lived, why should you let him handle the enormous responsibility of clearing your estate once you die? It is always more expensive to use a layman as an executor!

The best bargain you will ever receive from a bank is to use its Trust Department as your executor. The full-service bank's Trust Department has the experts. They know how to handle your estate, quickly, efficiently, and inexpensively.

Above all, don't die without a will! Husbands and wives generally cannot inherit from each other without a will. Most inheritances must go through the bloodline, unless there is a will that says otherwise. Husbands and wives are not heirs of the blood. If you want to protect your wife or husband, make a will and say so. All states have statutes which allow a little piece of your assets to pass to your spouse if you die without a will. This little piece is not enough. It is always expensive to administer an estate without a will. Wills save money! How much money they save depends on how intelligently your will is prepared. Make a formal will with expert help; name the Trust Department of your full-service bank as executor, and your estate will not be abused. There is no other way to guarantee the fast, efficient, expert handling of your estate.

Your old will could become expensive to use if it is more than five years old. Review your old will at least every five years to keep it current. That old will, if prepared in a different state than the one in which you now reside, probably can be used in your new state. However, your out-of-state will must be more expensive to use. The old will could violate the new state's law or, perhaps, mean something quite different in your new state. Always prepare a new will, with proper legal help, when you move to a new state.

PART FOUR
Probate

12

What Is Probate?

Almost every day, someone walks into my office and tells me he wants to avoid probate. When I ask if he knows what probate is, he says, "No." When I ask if he can afford to avoid probate, he doesn't know.

Bad advice in estate planning can make probate costly, just as bad advice on avoiding probate can. The important thing is to have expert legal advice for your personal situation.

Probate is the orderly passing of assets through court to your heirs according to the terms of a will. If you don't have a will, it is the orderly passing of assets through court according to the terms of your state's statute on descent and distribution.

There is *no law* that requires a probate. If you own nothing when you die, there is no probate whatsoever.

The way to avoid probate, and the *only* way to avoid

probate, is to divest yourself of your assets while you live.

In other words, in order to avoid probate, you must give away everything you own now. If done improperly, this can be very expensive and dangerous.

Probate guarantees that the people you *want* to inherit your assets will receive them in the least expensive manner, with minimum taxes, commissions, and fees. Should you recklessly adopt some of the side-door conveniences offered to the American public today, in any attempt to avoid probate you might do *yourself* serious harm!

Before we discuss when and how you should try to avoid probate, we must eliminate unwholesome, unnecessary, and foolish fears caused by failure to understand the reasons for probate.

People with assets use probate. The reasons are obvious. Few children know how to dispose of a parent's assets without family fights and misunderstandings. There are, of course, other basic reasons, such as enormous tax complications when you improperly avoid probate, and possible tax savings if you should not and don't avoid probate.

The executor or administrator, as the case may be, must do certain things to administer an estate.

People with assets generally cannot avoid probate. Probate-avoidance schemes will, perhaps, delay probate, if a husband or wife dies—until the surviving spouse dies. At that point, however, it is usually necessary to probate.

If you take time to properly plan your estate, probate is *not* expensive; it can save your estate money, especially in taxes.

A more immediate example is when you have real estate which has greatly appreciated during your lifetime. Your tax basis (what you paid for it) is low. If you sell it, you must pay a capital-gains tax. If you give it to your children, you will pay a gift tax based on its current fair market value on the day of the gift. However, that real estate will be given a step up in basis, for tax purposes, to its fair market value on the day of your death. If you die and probate it to your children, you save gift taxes, wipe out capital-gains taxes and give your children a new high-tax basis to help their capital-gains problems in the future. Only an estate planner (not a salesman) can tell you if the gift tax, inheritance tax, capital-gains tax, or estate tax will be best for you. Don't automatically discount probate, for it might be your best solution. Any of many tax considerations are your biggest problem today; not probate. Probate is only costly if you do not plan properly, or if you listen to bank clerks and commission salesmen rather than seek competent professional help in making estate-planning decisions. It strikes me as rather bad arithmetic to pay what can amount to a 5 to 35 percent capital-gains tax to save a 4 percent probate fee. The same is true of stock certificates that have appreciated in value.

No one with $100,000 or more should automatically try to avoid probate. This is the point where probate can become cheaper than paying taxes. If you have less than $100,000, you may well consider avoiding probate and turn to Part Six. If your total assets (and you usually should include your life insurance in this figure) exceed $100,000, you should *not* automatically try to avoid probate. You will not save money! You can lose much more than you save!

No one should attempt to save probate, regardless of their net worth, except a husband and wife who are both in a *first* marriage. In no other situation can probate be avoided without extreme danger. If you have a second marriage, and you use joint tenancy with your second spouse in order to avoid probate, you will suffer gift taxes, and you will automatically disinherit your children. Why? Because you would have given your new spouse a gift of the assets when you made them into joint tenancy, and you cannot give away jointly-owned property by will. Jointly-owned property, by definition, means that each of the joint tenants owns it all, and the first one to die loses the right to will any of it away. It belongs to the surviving joint-owner. If you attempt to use joint tenancy to avoid probate, gift taxes can exceed a probate fee; you also take the chance that creditors of your joint-owner will take the property away from you while you live.

13

How Probate Works

Your executor must see to it that proper legal petitions are prepared and that a hearing day in court is set. He must go to court with the attorney and explain why he should be appointed. The legal requirements for this are technical.

Timely notices and publications are always necessary. After the hearing, if your executor is appointed, he must then proceed to collect assets, prepare inventories, file proper, timely legal notice to creditors, prosecute and defend claims, make accountings, collect your assets, sell your assets, pay your bills, pay taxes, obtain tax waivers, make court appearances for permission to do various things, and ultimately prepare a final accounting and close the estate. The following is a partial list of an executor's duties and explanation of how an estate is handled. It should be clear to each of you that it is far too complicated for your son or daughter, if they are not knowledgeable in this field.

Your executor must do the following things:

1. Examine the will and note any special instructions. If there are no heirs living close by, the executor might also make funeral arrangements. The executor should then confer with the attorney who drew the will (if the will was so drawn) and with members of the family.

2. The next job of the executor is to safeguard the assets of the deceased and take whatever protective measures are necessary, even before his appointment in court as executor. This can be a very vital period. There are assets that might be wasting, that might perish, or that might disappear if they are not properly protected.

3. If you had a business, the executor must see to the continuation of the business, so that the business can either pass to your heirs or be sold in the administration of your estate for top dollar.

4. The executor must offer the will for probate to the appropriate probate court. He must retain the services of an attorney to prepare and file the necessary petitions, and set a hearing date in court.

5. The executor usually has a duty to publish a public notice in a newspaper of general circulation that an estate is going to be opened and a will offered for probate (an administrator will be appointed where there was no will). Legal notices say when and where the court hearing will take place. It invites all those

who are interested, or who wish to oppose the appointment of the executor or administrator, to come to court.

6. The executor must be present in court at the hearing and explain his qualifications to the Judge. This is a very important safeguard. The judge will then either appoint him executor or appoint an administrator. Once appointed, the executor takes over the active job of administering your estate. Should your executor become ill or die, the court would then, after another expensive legal proceeding, appoint an administrator. This is but one more reason why you should not use a human being as an executor. Your executor might be in jail when you die and your will is presented for probate. It is always safer to use the impartial expert—once again, the bank.

7. The executor must publish notice to creditors after his appointment, and all states have different time notices and different laws for how long a notice to creditors must run. It is necessary that notice to creditors be published in order to protect the business interests in your community. Many people have obligations which must be paid after death. If proper notice to creditors is ignored, your estate cannot close and lawsuits can develop, which will be very expensive. Amateur executors cannot be expected to handle these problems.

8. The executor must: Make an inventory of all assets. Collect all cash in the name of the deceased. Inventory all personal items that might have unique value. Collect life insurance payable to the estate, or assist the beneficiary named in the policy to collect the insurance.

Arrange for the supervision and management of any business interests. Obtain custody of securities. Collect interest and dividends. Review leases. Prosecute and defend claims. Check taxes and loans on any real estate, and arrange for the management of these properties.

All assets which you owned in a joint relationship with any of your relatives and friends must also be inventoried for tax purposes. Children often hide these assets, or refuse to cooperate with an executor, and this makes the probate much more expensive. This is but another reason why you should not use joint assets (joint tenancy) with children.

9. The executor will appraise all assets for federal estate tax purposes and/or for the tax requirements of the state where you lived. Obtaining the proper value on various holdings can be an exhausting and expensive affair. This is no place for an amateur. All assets are valued as of the date of death and again, perhaps, six months later, for more favorable tax advantages. Low values might offer estate-tax savings, but high values might produce income tax savings.

10. The executor must continue to administer the estate governed by the provisions of the will and the law of the last state where you were a resident. If there is no will, the administrator must follow that state's law for administrations; this is an additional complication and, once again, no place for an amateur. The executor and the administrator must give attention to business interests. They determine the policy of continuance, liquidation, or sale with due regard to the wishes of the

deceased. They consider the wishes of the family and the family's needs. This surely is no area for the uninitiated.

It takes an individual with great expertise to make correct decisions. The executor must also review the assets and cash requirements for administrative costs, taxes, and the like. If the estate is nonliquid, he will decide which assets shall be sold for immediate funds. He must decide if real estate is to be sold, obtain the proper asking price, and make the correct sales arrangements. If no sale is necessary, the executor must attend to the production of the highest possible income from this real estate and negotiate leases. The executor must determine and investigate all claims of creditors. The claims must either be approved or rejected, and there are certain specific legal requirements for the manner of these acceptances or rejections. Any errors made in this area can be expensive. The executor must then present the claims he accepts to the court for court approval, before payment. This, of course, is for your benefit and for the benefit of your heirs.

11. The executor must now determine and settle taxes. This is a highly complicated and technical procedure. It involves numerous choices and options which may be used to reduce both income and estate taxes. Estates pay income taxes, just as a living individual does. There are options for reporting income. In some cases, the income should be reported by the estate. In other cases, it is advantageous to report the income in the tax of the deceased for the year during which he

died. These choices require a great amount of knowledge and expertise.

The executor must file your income tax returns for
that part of the year prior to your death. Other income
tax returns, known as "Fiduciary Returns," must also
be filed for the balance of the year in which you died
and your estate was opened. The executor must review
all returns and assist in their preparation. In the estate
tax area, the executor must file timely notices in both
the federal and state tax departments. Improper filing
can cause penalties and interest. He must then prepare
and file the estate-tax return. Obviously, the services
of an expert will be required in most instances; a competent executor will know where to get proper advice.
The executor is personally responsible for any errors he
makes.

12. After all of the foregoing has been completed,
the executor must prepare the final accounting. This
consists of a detailed statement of receipts and disburse-
ments which will be presented to the court. A date must
be set for another hearing, proper petitions must be
filed, and notices of such a hearing must be made available to all who are entitled to such notice. Errors made
at this point are expensive. A layman usually cannot
prepare a proper accounting. He certainly cannot prepare an accounting in the most inexpensive and advantageous manner to your estate.

13. After court approval, the executor must distribute the estate. This, once again, requires an impartial
expert. A supplemental accounting to the court and
filing of receipts from the beneficiaries will be necessary.

At that time, a final discharge of the executor or administrator can be obtained from the court.

In my jurisdiction, all of this can be done in four months. If your estate is taxable, the federal government can audit the estate, and this might take a bit longer. If you have a taxable estate, there are options which an expert may exercise. Assets can be valued at two different times. There are disadvantages and advantages in choosing one valuation date over another.

Don't think you can avoid these taxes by avoiding probate. If you eliminate probate because you have given your assets away through one of the various methods of avoiding probate, tax returns must still be filed. And this is a real mess!

A blanket statement that you should do one thing or another, without explaining some of the pitfalls resulting, is as dangerous as getting straight-out, inaccurate advice. *You must learn to protect yourself.* Anytime you read a statement that says everyone should categorically take one action or another, without proper explanation, you must be very careful. Not everyone should probate, but not everyone—most assuredly—can afford to avoid probate. Inaccurate information on this subject, which does not explain the dangers in joint property or the problems relating to probate avoidance, will cause many of you serious distress. You must exercise extreme caution, and get your own legal advice from your own attorney, if you are to avoid probate safely.

One dangerous area usually ignored by those who tell you to avoid probate is estate taxation. Your estate will be taxable and subject to a United States federal estate tax, if everything you own exceeds the value of $60,000. By "everything," I mean all real estate, wherever located; stocks; bonds; investments; checking accounts; savings accounts; time certificates of deposit; personal property; automobiles; jewelry; and, more often than not, the full value of your life insurance. Life insurance, as you have been previously informed, can be removed from your taxable estate, but only with the help of an expert.

If your estate is less than $100,000 and you are in a first marriage, it might be both possible and cheaper for you to avoid probate through joint tenancy. The tax you will pay does not usually justify using probate simply to avoid taxes. It may be much more convenient to pay a modest tax.

If your estate is more than $100,000, other considerations apply. The federal estate tax is a "Progressive Tax," which means that the more money you have, the higher the tax percentage you must pay. Over $100,000, your taxes begin to greatly exceed any conceivable probate fee.

If you abuse your estate by naming an incompetent executor, or if you name someone who does not have the time to handle the job properly, you might as well take out your checkbook now. Enormous sums of money are wasted by inexperienced executors. This waste is usually inadvertent but, nevertheless, it occurs. And the inability of your executor to inexpensively administer *your* estate is *your* fault!

14

The Executor

If you name a relative in Boston to administer an estate when you live in Southern California, you can't expect him to walk to California to do the job. There will be expensive airplane fares (first-class no doubt), motel rooms, ground transportation, and living expenses. It is impossible to inexpensively administer an estate long-distance. It is absurd to name an executor who is not a resident in the community where you live.

It is certainly not the fault of what is normally an efficient, effective legal process if you complicate it by intentionally naming an executor without knowledge or experience.

Probate is one area where you cannot afford to bypass an expert. It is always cheaper to have an expert, like a trust company or the Trust Department of a full-service bank, or your attorney, handle your estate. If you have no faith in your attorney, he should not be your attorney. If you don't have any faith in the Trust Department of your bank, you should not be doing business with that bank. Consider the tremendous savings for your heirs if you wisely and responsibly name a competent executor.

In my state, an uninformed legislator recently prevailed and sponsored a bill which was passed and written into law. This bill says: "That a nonresident can be the executor in an estate no matter where he lives." In other words, it is no longer necessary in Arizona that an executor for a resident of Arizona also reside in the state of Arizona. Many of my clients have since rushed back to my office. They are delighted. They say, "We can now name our own dear child to handle the administration of our estate." This always appalls me. I ask these individuals whether or not they understand what an executor must do. They don't! I ask them if they know anything about the availability of their relative when they die. They don't! Their standard answer is, "Oh, he'll [or she'll] be glad to do it for me."

Unfortunately, you can't run your business in one state while you live in another unless it is large enough to have expert managers. What makes you think that your executor can handle your estate from another jurisdiction? He most certainly *cannot!* The executor must do all of the things previously mentioned in this section. They must be done in the state in which you last resided. The court appearances in the state where you last lived will require that your executor and his attorney be there. In other words, these nonresident

3333

executors might go back and forth three to four times in order to get the job done properly. Just think of the outrageous expense. Your executor may come out here, stay at the best hotels, have a wonderful vacation, and bill it all to your estate. It has happened more than once!

My trust officer, who is an associate and an employee in my law firm, was recently presented bills exceeding $2,300 by the executors of a deceased person. They came out to Arizona with their families and had a wonderful vacation. They stayed at one of our top resort hotels and ate well, among other things. I refused to present these bills to the court. They are upset. They are nowhere near as upset as the other heirs would be, had I accepted such bills. The remaining heirs demand that the fun and frolic of your executor not be paid by your estate.

Your executor will demand that all of his expenses be paid, because he was obliged to come in and administer your estate. Many problems will develop in Arizona because our uneducated legislator did not properly analyze the bill he pushed through the legislature. He was trying to impress his constituents. Too bad they don't know the damage he has done their estates. Don't abuse your assets! Name an executor who is a resident of the state where you reside. Anything else must, by its very nature, be too expensive!

Don't blame the probate system for the disaster you cause! You, if you name an incompetent, nonresident relative or other person, create your own disasters!

Finally, it has been my experience that quite often an out-of-state executor simply renounces his appointment. He refuses to serve. He cannot afford the time away from his own business and family. When that happens, the court must appoint an administrator, and that is always a more expensive route to take.

15

The Cost of Probate

Probate need not be costly. You, and no one but you, determine the cost. In my state, the fees have been approximately 4 percent. Our new statute should not result in substantially different fees. Generally, in all states, if you spend the time and a few dollars to have a proper estate plan and a valid will prepared by a competent attorney, you will save money. The executor's fee can be cut to a minimum. As a general rule, it can range from 2 percent to 6 percent. It is entirely possible that a valid estate plan will keep you in the lower portion of the fee range no matter where you reside.

In addition to the executor's fee, there will always be an attorney's fee. In most instances, the attorney's fee will be the same as the executor's. It can, however, be less, and at times it can be more. It is always more when you write your own will, or name a person who lives out of state as executor. Such actions always increase the lawyer's workload.

There is a very easy way to minimize probate costs. If you want to name a relative as executor merely because you want the personal or family involvement, do so. However, if you name a relative and your attorney (assuming he is an estate lawyer and knows what he is doing) as *coexecutors,* enormous savings are available. (The banks, naturally, never tell you about this.) In this manner, your attorney can do all the work and mail it to your coexecutor for approval. In other words, your lawyer coexecutor can do nothing without the consent of his coexecutor, that member of your family. The law requires that *all* coexecutors sign and consent to everything. This will relieve your relative from all the difficult work (for which he is generally unqualified). It will also save expensive travel costs, since your relative will not have to fly back and forth many times to do the work. When you name your lawyer and a relative as coexecutors, be sure to state in the will, itself, that the lawyer must take but *one fee!* He must accept the executor's or the lawyer's fee, but not both! You should also state that your relative will receive no fee. This is particularly true if your relative is the beneficiary. If he takes a fee, he will pay income tax on it. If he inherits it, he will not pay tax (unless the state has an inheritance tax). In this way, your estate is expertly handled, and your relative is fully involved. There is, however, only one fee. It should never exceed 4 percent, or the one statutory executor's fee allowable in the state where you reside.

SUMMARY OF PART FOUR

Probate is not an evil! It need not be expensive. It can save you money! Probate is simply the easiest, most efficient method of transferring your assets from one generation to another, or to whoever you name. It is done under the direction and with the approval of a court. This prevents your assets from disappearing. This prevents your children from fighting. This prevents you from losing your assets while you live in a reckless probate-avoidance situation. It is an efficient system, used by worldly people with any type of reasonable assets.

Only the unintelligent, the uninformed, and the uneducated attempt to avoid probate, without adequate knowledge of what it is. If you question the stories of disasters relating to "probate," you will find, in most cases, that the executors were generally incompetent. You will *rarely* find that a probate lawyer or the Trust Department of a full-service bank is an executor in those disastrously handled estates.

There is no law that requires probate. If you own nothing when you die, there is no probate. The only way to avoid probate is to give your assets away while you live. This can be dangerous! It can wipe you out!

You might not yet fully realize that you may be giving your assets away. You should realize it, once you read the Part entitled "Probate-Avoidance Tools." If you prepare a proper will, name a competent executor, and have your affairs in good order when you die, your probate will be quick, inexpensive, and save your heirs some disagreeable arguments.

Probate costs can be reasonable. They only become abusive if you have a bad will or name an incompetent executor. If you want to name a relative as executor, for reasons of sentiment, do so, and name your attorney as coexecutor with your relative. The attorney can do all the work.

Both coexecutors must sign all papers. While your attorney coexecutor can do all the work in the state where you live and die, he must always have the consent and approval of your relative coexecutor.

If you name a relative and your attorney as coexecutors, always state in the will, itself, that there is to be but one fee, and that the lawyer shall receive it. State that your attorney must accept only one (executor's or lawyer's) fee. In this manner, your estate will not pay a double fee.

PART FIVE
Trusts

16

The Anatomy of a Trust

Trusts are not new. They were used in antiquity. There are records of trusts in the Common Law as far back as 1500 A.D. There are different kinds of trusts. In this Part, we consider the "Living" or "Inter Vivos Trust" and the "Testamentary Trust." These are the two trusts which most of you probably mean when you say trust.

You do not have a trust when you use savings account and bank account "trusts." These are not anything like a true trust. These are a gimmick, which we will explain later. Husbands and wives must plan all trusts together. Each has a duty to tell the other what he is doing, and also a right to know what the other is doing. After all, each must live with that trust once the other is dead. If you are the beneficiary, you have the duty to tell your spouse what you want, and what your needs are. You must say whether or not you can live with what is going into that trust. If you haven't done it already, now is the time to do it. Once you are a widow or a widower, it is too late to change.

Much of the wealth in this country is controlled by trusts. Large family fortunes are administered in trusts. The trust is an ancient, efficient, effective vehicle in which to handle substantial assets. It is the proper way to minimize taxes. Many competent banks will not take a trust if the assets in trust are less than $100,000 to $500,000. These are the honest banks. They know the expenses involved and don't want to abuse your beneficiary with excessive minimum fees. A trust is *not* cheap. A trust can limit free use of property. It is no field for the layman. Trust forms are more vicious and dangerous than will forms. A trust must fit your needs and taxable estate carefully and exactly. It must carefully consider the needs and requirements of your beneficiary. Most new trust salesmen, selling nothing but trusts, rarely go into the needs of your beneficiary. Banks in areas where there are many retired people hire "new business salesmen" to go after new trust business. Too few of them are lawyers, and most of them have no tax background. Very few of them have had any experience with what happens at death when the beneficiary must *live* with the trust.

A living or inter vivos trust and a testamentary trust are quite similar. The basic difference is that a living trust is activated while you live, and a testamentary trust, while similar in other ways, is prepared and established in your will but does not become active until after you die. Many "new business salesmen" at banks say that they don't "believe" in the testamentary trust. I don't blame them. They don't get paid for their work on testamentary trusts until after the death of person who establishes it. A testamentary trust is for the benefit of somebody else. You don't make a testamentary trust for yourself. A living trust is usually for your benefit, although it can also be set up for the benefit of somebody else. It can have many beneficiaries, one following another, when the former dies.

Otherwise, in this chapter, what I write about a living trust will, essentially, apply to the testamentary trust. Any significant differences between the two will be explained. Later chapters will deal with each in detail.

Generally speaking, a trust relationship is a "Fiduciary" relationship. A fiduciary is a person who works with another person's money. A corporation (like a bank) can also be a fiduciary. A stockbroker can be a fiduciary, but please don't ever make one your executor or trustee. A fiduciary relationship allows someone to hold, use, and invest your assets for your benefit.

In other words, a trustee (a fiduciary) holds the assets of another person and is the legal owner of this property. The trustee, however, holds it for the benefit and use of somebody else. Simply put, you give your assets away when you put them in trust.

A trust is a contract. You agree to give what you own to the "trustee"; the trustee agrees to hold it and use it for your benefit, or the benefit of someone you name.

The trustee is now the owner, but the trustee is not the owner for himself. The trustee is the owner for you, or for whoever you wish to name as beneficiary. Therefore, when someone owns something as a trustee, *the trustee cannot use it for his own purposes*, without committing a crime or breaking the contract. If the trustee dies, the trust assets are not in his estate for tax purposes. They do not pass under his will. He cannot give the trust assets away. This is understandable. He did not own them for himself. If he becomes ill, a new trustee will be appointed. You might say a trustee is the legal owner, but it is less than complete ownership. He owns it only for the benefit of the beneficiary, who is the equitable or true owner.

To create a living trust, a lengthy trust document should be prepared by a competent estate planner. Some banks offer to prepare the trust document for you at no charge. This is no bargain. It is a disaster. It is almost criminal. The bank can abuse you. The bank will give itself too many powers, and you will suffer greatly. There are a variety of living and testamentary trusts. In all trusts, the duties and liabilities of the parties should be discussed in detail. You must know what assets you put into trust. The trustee must understand what he will own and be expected to do for your benefit. You both should understand what the duties and obligations of the trustee will be. The trustee must be paid, and occasionally will explain the total costs in advance. Trusts are *not* inexpensive. A trust is not a money-saving device. When you establish a living trust, you take something you own and give it to the trustee. The trustee can sell it, manage it, invest it, maintain it, whatever the case may be. He then pays the income and dividends to you, if the trust was established for your benefit. The trustee will, of course, do the same thing for a different beneficiary, if you established the trust for someone else.

The trustee owes a personal duty to the beneficiary. The beneficiary can enforce it in court, if necessary. The title to the trust property must be split. In the eyes of the law, the trustee holds the empty, legal title; the beneficiary is the owner of the equitable title. Equitable title is the stronger title. This gives any beneficiary the right to force the trustee to do things in his behalf, as established under the terms and conditions of the written trust agreement. If the trustee fails to do his job for the benefit of the beneficiary, the beneficiary who owns the equitable title can go to court and force the trustee either to resign or to do his job properly. This is one reason why you should never allow the bank to prepare your trust instrument for you. The bank certainly will not give you the maximum rights your own lawyer would put into the contract or trust instrument for you. I don't mean to imply that the banks necessarily or deliberately mislead you; it is just that some bank trust officers seem to believe that they deserve more power than they truly need.

When you establish a trust, you must be very specific. What you want done must be *carefully* explained and detailed into the trust instrument. If you do anything less than this, it is possible that expensive lawsuits will result.

In the past seven or eight years, the living trust has become the most abused, dissipated, expensive tool for every irresponsible and unknowledgeable financial sales person in America. They sell living trusts as a probate avoidance, hence as a savings device. One would think they were selling a baloney sandwich.

A trust does *not* truly save a probate fee! Let me repeat: A living trust does *not* truly save a probate fee! A living trust *replaces* the probate fee with a trustee's fee. The trustee's fee can certainly be more expensive in the long run than the probate fee. Economy should not persuade you to avoid a trust, if a trust is what you need.

There are many valid reasons for a living trust. Some of them are:

1. You are not incompetent, but just forgetful.

2. You are ill and cannot handle your financial affairs.

3. You need help to care for yourself.

4. Your assets are so complicated, and your investments so varied, that it is now beyond your ability to handle them.

5. You are retired and don't want to be bothered with playing the market or handling investments.

6. You have a large amount of cash, and you don't want to waste it by having it shrink in a savings-and-loan account. You want it invested by an expert.

7. You want your assets to be used for the benefit of a minor child or another unknowledgeable person, who

does not have the ability or capacity to invest it properly and safely.

8. You seek some of the tax advantages available through trusts.

9. You want to provide security and safety for a spouse if you die.

There are substantially the identical estate tax advantages in the use of a testamentary trust (a trust under your will) as in a living trust. A living trust might offer some income tax advantages which a testamentary trust might not.

There are people who need a trust. Many husbands should consider the advantages of testamentary trusts in their wills when they provide for their widows.

If you decide that you can afford and will benefit from a living trust, or a testamentary trust, always name a trustee in the community where you live. Put a clause into all trusts that the "income beneficiary" can ask the trustee to resign and nominate a Trust Department in a bank in the community of residence if the beneficiary must move to another city. No trusts that I have ever seen prepared by a bank had this clause in it.

It is foolhardy to name a trustee in a distant place. I had one Arizona client who had prepared a trust naming a New York City bank as trustee. I suggested he change it. He was convinced that his former lawyer had done the proper thing.

He is now dead. The trust is now irrevocable, and his wife is the unhappy beneficiary. Her long-distance telephone bills are enormous.

You need your trustee close by for many reasons. You

should be able to go to your trust administrator quickly and bang on his desk, if you are unhappy. Your wife should be able to look him in the eye at any time and say, "Okay, son, tell me why not . . ."

It takes a Ph.D in geometry to understand some of the quarterly computer printouts these banks use. A beneficiary will want to be able to conveniently have them explained. There will be many other problems which require personal communication. It is unrealistic to imagine that your beneficiary will receive the same service from a long-distance trustee that a local trustee will provide.

17

The Inter Vivos or Living Trust

The inter vivos or living trust is a trust whereby you take your assets, give them to the bank, and name the bank as trustee; the bank will invest, manage, hold, protect, and distribute your assets. The bank will pay your bills, give you the income accruing, and generally make your retired life extremely comfortable. I refer to the bank as trustee because I am trying to impress on you the fact that in my opinion only an honest bank should be your trustee. Most living trusts are revocable. You can end them or take out any amount of money at any time. It is distressing when a client insists upon naming a child as trustee. Children generally know less about the investment of money and the handling of your assets than you do. Often, they also don't have time to give the trust the attention it needs.

The supreme advantage offered by a living trust is that your assets will be invested by a group of experts. Hopefully, they will hedge against inflation. You will thus have a secure retirement and not dissipate your assets unnecessarily. In addition, you would want the money to be spent for your benefit if this should become necessary. I have had occasion to be disappointed in the very slow manner in which some son-or-daughter trustees invade principal for the benefit of their parents, who are the sole beneficiaries of their own living trusts. In order to guarantee that you receive all your living trust benefits, you should name an expert as trustee. A trust company or the Trust Department at an honest bank is where this expert may be found.

All trustees will be paid. Banks, just as any other business, are profit-oriented. They do not work for nothing. They must be paid; they expect to be paid; they are entitled to be paid for their services. The services do not come cheaply. There is an annual fee. There is a minimum fee. There is a withdrawal fee. There is a termination fee at death. However, they are a bargain, if you do need a living trust.

Unfortunately, some Trust Department new business salesmen are so anxious to receive your money and put it into a trust that they neglect to draw a proper distinction between those who can afford a trust and those who cannot.

There are also attorneys so anxious to earn a fee drafting trusts—and so anxious to avoid offending the bank which sends them trust business—that they don't accurately analyze the cost features for you. You have to protect yourself!

Today, many banks in the United States earn high profits from their living trusts. With such high-profit potential, it's small wonder that the Trust Departments push trusts and, in their enthusiasm, don't dwell on the costs. The Trust Departments talk about annual trust fees. These fees are a percentage of the trust assets. Many Trust Departments charge a yearly percentage of the entire amount of money in trust. Some charge a higher percentage on only the income which the trust earns. Trust fees, generally, approximate something like 6/10 of 1 percent, which is comparatively inexpensive. It is, indeed, a modest charge for those who need a living trust. Some Trust Departments charge 4/10 of 1 percent, but have an annual minimum fee of $500 to $1,000 as base, and charge 4/10 of 1 percent on everything thereafter. In any event, 6/10 of 1 percent, or $6.00 per $1,000, based upon everything in the trust, is something entirely different when you compare it to the income accruing.

Let's assume you have $100,000 in trust. Further, let's assume that the annual fee of $6.00 per $1,000 or 6/10 of 1 percent would be $600 per year. Now assume that you have the extraordinary good fortune of a trust that pays 6 percent, so that your accruing income would be $6,000 per year. The annual trust fee of $600 will be taken out of the $6,000 income. That means you pay 10 percent of your income as your trustee's annual fee. If the trust has an annual minimum fee of $1,000, you will

pay 16.66 percent of your income to the trustee as an annual fee. You can see clearly that a trust is not cheap. In
addition, most Trust Departments charge you 1 percent
for any monies you take out of trust. Regrettably, very
few new business salesmen in Trust Departments mention this withdrawal fee. In other words, if you invade
the principal and take back any of the monies you placed
into trust, there may be a 1 percent charge. There is also
a 1 percent termination fee at the time when the trust
is terminated, or at your death. Trust fees are varied
and negotiable; you should always bargain.

It should now be obvious, even to the most uninformed reader, that a trust does not truly "save" a probate fee. It replaces one probate fee after you die, with
a yearly trustee's fee. Over the years, the annual trustee's
fee should add up to more than a probate fee. It is for
this reason that I say a living trust should *never* be used
to avoid probate, if there is no other valid reason for
the trust.

On the other hand, if you have any of the many valid
reasons for this beautiful vehicle, then you get the
added benefit of no probate. However, no probate
should be considered only an incidental benefit of the
trust. Unfortunately, too many trusts are sold by enthusiastic new trust officers for no reason whatsoever,
other than to save a probate fee. This is not good economics!

I am an enthusiastic supporter and user of the living
trust. I recommend it to the vast majority of my clients
who have sufficient assets and a need for a living trust.

However, all Trust Departments have a minimum fee. A minimum fee is reasonable and necessary for them to stay in business. Make sure you understand how much you will pay each year, in dollars, and what percentage of the trust income it equals.

The trust vehicle works quite simply. You give your assets to the trustee. He becomes the legal owner. You remain the equitable owner, and he must use the assets for your benefit. While you live, you *can* direct his investments. This is called a "Directed" living trust. I don't usually recommend this to most of my clients, since I believe that the retired, and people of advanced age, have no business being in the marketplace. I certainly don't believe that most widows should be playing around in the market. If you are going to have a living trust, take advantage of the expertise in the Trust Department of your trust company or bank. Let them handle the investments.

Another abused area: Say you have good securities, and the Trust Department automatically sells them and purchases shares for your benefit into various common trust funds. Most Trust Departments in large banks have a variety of common trust funds. They are not unlike mutual funds. They are certainly a well-run, conservative type of investment. There is nothing wrong with them. Most people would be in a better position if their assets were there. Nevertheless, the banks make enormous profits on these common trust funds. It should not cost them five cents extra to have one million or ten million dollars in these trust funds. They don't have to work hard, in effect, for their fee, if they keep your assets in these common trust funds. Generally, you still pay a full trust fee, whether you are in a common trust fund or whether they handle your trust account as a separate investment fund. A few banks seem to have had an attack of conscience, and recently some of them are starting to charge lower fees.

If you have good securities that provide sufficient income and reasonable growth, there is often no reason to sell them, simply in order to put you into a common trust fund. When they are sold, capital-gains tax must often be paid. Many banks don't inform you of this until after the fact. If you have good investments and set up a living trust, you must direct the trustee bank *not* to sell your assets without your consent, and *not* to automatically place you into a common trust fund.

Every individual, at a certain stage in his life or beyond a certain age, if he has substantial assets (and, by substantial assets, I mean something in excess of $100,000), might benefit from some type of a living trust. Exactly when this point is reached can only be determined by your individual circumstances and your physical and emotional stability. If you don't have enough money to generate sufficient income to meet the annual minimum charge of a trust, then it is simply not good economics to have a living trust. Some (new) trust businessmen, in their enthusiasm, do not understand this point.

Assume that you have good investments, secure investments, blue-chip securities, and your health is fairly good. There would seem to be no reason for you, at this stage, to have a living trust. You are, nevertheless, the person who should seriously consider a testamentary trust under your will for the benefit of your spouse or other heir.

Many widows might feel more secure with a testamentary trust. Once again, this is a matter of economics; you should first consider whether or not you have sufficient assets to place what you own into a trust for your heirs.

If you have any of the valid reasons for a living trust, then you cannot concern yourself with costs. The price you pay will be a bargain. Your assets will be preserved, and you will be well maintained. This is only, of course, if you use a full-service Trust Department at a full-service bank or a trust company as trustee.

You should never have a living trust with a mutual-funds company as trustee. I tell you why in great detail in Chapter 23: "The Pseudo-Trust That Is Not a Trust."

It is equally imprudent to have a trust with your relative as trustee. Recently a lady visited me who had established a trust with $120,000 in cash and blue-chip stocks. She had named her son-in-law as trustee. "After all, he was a businessman," she told me. This businessman dissipated the trust. He more than dissipated it. He destroyed it. He used some of the assets for his own personal affairs and, of course, he lost them. He tried to make spectacular profits in order to replace the money; this reckless speculation caused even more losses so that, ultimately, the total assets this lady owned were less than $20,000. She could sue him, but he is her son-in-law. He is also broke. Don't you take such foolish chances! If you need a living trust, use a trust company or the Trust Department of your full-service bank as trustee. That is where experts will properly handle your affairs. If they commit errors that a reasonably prudent trustee would not commit, they have substantial assets behind them, and you can sue and collect for damages.

If you name an individual as trustee, and he abuses or absconds with your money, there is usually no chance to recover your losses. If you want to be safe, never, never, absolutely *never,* make a living trust with anyone except a trustee in the Trust Department of your full-service bank or a trust company. Should you do otherwise, it is often an invitation to disaster!

There are a variety of living trusts. Many individuals, with excellent credentials, believe that the testamentary trust (Chapter 18), is becoming less useful. However, it still has an important place in estate planning. This is especially true for those who are not completely retired or who want to protect a surviving spouse.

There is a comparatively new type of living trust that is very popular and practical. This is called an "Un-funded" living trust. Some people refer to it as a "standby" living trust. This living trust is exactly like any other living trust except that you will not put anything into this trust now. An unfunded living trust is often funded with life-insurance policies on the life of the trustor, so it is actually not truly funded. There is, of course, no annual trustee's charge for such a trust, so long as it is unactivated and unfunded. Many individuals will create such a living trust and fund it with $10 or $20, just to put it in existence on the bank's books, awaiting emergencies.

The utility, validity, and appeal of such a trust is obvious. If you become ill, the trust is there, and you can fund it at once without delay. This is a most efficient and highly recommended estate-planning tool. The security and peace of mind you will enjoy from this kind of trust often removes a lot of worry. Should your assets become a burden to you, simply fund this trust. It is efficient, it is fast, it is a highly recommended trust vehicle.

An unfunded living trust requires that you spend some money today for benefits you hope to receive in the future. Many retired individuals don't like to spend money unnecessarily. On the other hand, this should not stop you from seriously considering an unfunded living trust if you do have assets, and you believe that the burden of maintaining them will increase through the years. The obvious advantage of such a trust becomes apparent should you become ill. If you then fund this existing trust, and your illness is fatal, your widow would have the advantage of the living trust already in existence. Your widow would not have to wait for the administration of the estate to have the trust funded. I believe any retired person, with assets, can probably benefit from an unfunded trust.

18

The Testamentary Trust

A testamentary trust works almost exactly like a living trust. The basic difference is that you make the trust instrument in and as a part of your will. Thus, the trust does not go into effect until after you die. You will not pay an annual trustee's fee while you live. Once you die, and your estate is administered, your assets will pass into the trust. The bank will be the trustee, and whoever you name will be the beneficiary. At this point, after your estate is closed, the trustee's annual fee will commence.

The testamentary trust is a most underrated vehicle. It should be used more! During 12 years of practice in a retirement community, it has been demonstrated to me that many widows benefit from testamentary trusts.

The shock of being alone after a lengthy and happy marriage continues for a long time. Many widows never completely recover. Few of them know how to make investments, or how to manage the investments they already own. Nothing is stable in the marketplace. Many good stocks this year are bad stocks next year. It is presumptuous of you to assume that your widow, or other beneficiary, will necessarily have access to proper advice. In such a case, probably the best thing you can do is establish a testamentary trust under your will. Your beneficiary can then continue to carry on normal activities without the burden of money management.

Too many of my widowed clients make imprudent, reckless, and absurd investments. One, recently, actually purchased a mortgage from a scoundrel disguised as a cleric. He told her he was selling secure second mortgages. She took her entire cash savings and purchased a mortgage that was to pay her 16 percent interest a year. She couldn't resist; the income potential was so enormous, and he was, "after all," she told me, "a man of the cloth." He wasn't even an honest man, much less a man of the cloth. He also did not own the real estate on which he allegedly sold the mortgage. She lost everything! This is not a unique case among confused, elderly widows.

If you have a wife, once you establish a testamentary trust for her, everything you place into the trust will not be probated at her death. When she dies, the assets in the trust will not be taxed to her estate.

There are substantial tax advantages in both living and testamentary trusts. All these advantages might not help you, but they inure to the benefit of your children. When we die, each of us is subject to a United States

federal estate tax. The tax begins on estates of $60,000.
As a practical matter, I inform my clients that they
need *not* worry about the tax unless they have more
than $100,000. The tax is based upon the transfer of
ownership of assets as the result of a death. In other
words, if you own a block of stock, and this stock trans-
fers ownership to your spouse or your heir as a result
of your death, this transfer is what is taxed. There is,
therefore, no way to avoid the estate tax if we own more
than $60,000 of taxable assets when we die. However,
the tax is not abusive up to $100,000. A married person
who dies usually will not pay any tax up to $120,000.

Any monies we place into a trust for ourselves—such
as a living trust—are subject to a tax at our death. Most
living trusts are revocable, and give income to the
trustor. It is for this reason that anything we put into a
revocable living trust is taxed to us or against our estate
when we die. If we control the trust, then we control
the assets in the trust. If we can revoke the trust, then
we regain control of the assets. This is enough to establish the tax. You do not, therefore, save any federal
estate taxes on your death by putting assets you own
into a revocable living trust. There can, however, be
income tax advantages.

On the other hand, assets you place into a testamentary trust for the benefit of a different person other than
yourself—such as your wife, will not be probated when
that beneficiary dies; these assets also will not be taxed
to that beneficiary's estate when he or she dies.

In other words, if you place something into a testamentary trust for the benefit of your *wife,* and in that trust you state: "When my wife dies, this trust shall terminate, and this property shall pass to my children or remain in trust for my children," the passage of the assets happens automatically at her death. Since she was only a beneficiary and had the *equitable* ownership, not the *legal* ownership, these assets will *not* be taxed to her when she dies. She never owned them. She never had legal title. Ownership or title to these assets did not pass to another person by virtue of *her* death. The ownership passed, ultimately, by virtue of *your* death. Therefore, they won't be taxed at her death.

There are substantial tax savings to your heirs in the use of a testamentary trust. If the beneficiary is someone other than the person who set up the trust, the beneficiary will not be taxed for the trust assets when he or she dies. In other words, if you leave your assets to your wife as owner without a trust when you die, then she becomes the owner. When she dies, subsequent to you, everything will be probated and taxed. Had you placed these assets into a testamentary trust under your will for her benefit, when she dies, nothing will be probated, and nothing in the trust will be taxed to her estate.

A final word concerning the drafting of all trust instruments. Make sure that you do not tie your spouse's hands so that he or she might lose control of your family. Too many trusts are mere forms, copied by one who is not interested enough to draft the exact trust to fit your individual needs. These form trusts don't have the flexibility that a beneficiary should enjoy. Many widows complain to me that they haven't seen the children or grandchildren for some years. They explain that their husbands established a trust for their benefit, while he was alive or under his will. When they die, all of the assets from the trust automatically go to the children or grandchildren. The children and the grandchildren know this, and they often seem to have less time for Grandmother. Consider the consequences of tying your spouse's hands this way.

It might appall you to know how often I receive such complaints. They are most frequent when a son and/or daughter dies young and the son-in-law or daughter-in-law remarries and allows the grandchildren to grow up remote from the grandparent concerned.

These problems can be avoided if you give your widow or widower the right to include in his or her will the distribution of the trust as he or she sees fit among a selected class of your heirs. This is called "power of appointment." It means that your widow or widower can, at any time in the future, change his or her will and state: "Under my spouse's trust or under that trust he (or she) established in my behalf, I have the right to give away these assets after my death. I give these assets away in the following manner . . ." I don't recommend that my clients use this power unless they feel that it is absolutely necessary. It involves various tax consequences which are too technical and complicated to explain here. But this simple little device may prevent a widow from ever being lonely.

19

*Powers and Duties
of a Trustee, and
Rights of a Beneficiary*

Many people are afraid of trusts simply because they don't quite understand them. They believe that in establishing a trust they lose all control of their property. This is not so! A trustee is a fiduciary. He owns the trust property for your benefit, if you are the beneficiary. The trustee does not own the trust assets for himself.

The trustee must not act as the "owner" of assets held in trust. He must act as a "reasonably prudent man," exclusively and solely for the benefit of the beneficiary.

The trust instrument, which is a legal document, should be prepared by your lawyer. Don't allow the trustee bank to prepare the trust for you; this is false economy. It is quite improper for any bank to act as a lawyer and prepare trust instruments. Nevertheless, many banks are guilty of this abuse. It is false economy if you allow them to prepare the trust instrument. They do not protect you quite as much as your own attorney. They might well give themselves too much power. They might well not give you the flexibility you deserve and the rights you should have in your own trust. Have your own attorney prepare the trust instrument—assuming, of course, that he is a qualified tax estate planner.

Once the trust instrument is prepared and explained to you by your independent attorney, it must then be approved by the trustee bank. If the trust is approved, the trustor (you) and the trustee (the bank) both sign the document, and it becomes a valid contract. You are protected by the law of contract, and certain duties and obligations will vest against the trustee. If violation of these duties occurs, you can sue.

Next, you deliver the trust assets to the trustee, and these assets are put into the trustee's name as legal owner. The beneficiary—and in most living trusts it is oneself, the trustor—will retain the equitable ownership. You can clearly see that no one can force a trust upon you. You must sign a trust document in the same manner as you sign any other formal contract.

The creation of a testamentary trust is quite similar. You simply incorporate the formal trust document into your will. You cannot force this trust upon a bank, but assuming it was prepared by a competent tax-trained estate planner, most banks will accept the trust if there is a reasonable amount of money involved.

The duties, rights, and liabilities of the parties are protected by law. Generally speaking, you can revoke a living trust if you were the trustor, unless you made it irrevocable in the beginning. You can also modify and change the trust. The trustee will usually agree to, and accept, your change, unless it is illegal or most imprudent. The important thing to remember is that the trustee does have the right to refuse your change; if he does refuse, you can always revoke the trust and take back all of your assets. The trustee has a duty to invest the trust assets in accordance with good business practices. He must give all the income it earns to you, or spend the income for your benefit. He must do the same for any beneficiary. The trustee must use all of the principal, and spend it for your benefit, if the income produced is not enough to maintain you. All of these things must be spelled out in the trust agreement itself.

There is little reason ever to use an irrevocable living trust. The one exception that I suggest is a life insurance trust for your life insurance if you are sure you will not need the policies for loans, security, or other purposes. By making a life insurance trust irrevocable, and naming your spouse and children as beneficiaries, you will completely remove this asset from your taxable estate. This can mean substantial estate tax savings at your death.

In testamentary trusts established under your will, the first beneficiary is usually your spouse. The spouse generally cannot revoke, amend, or alter that trust in any way. It is for this reason that you should first communicate with the beneficiary of your testamentary trust and make sure you understand what his or her needs and wishes are; allow for them in the trust. The trustee of a testamentary trust, nevertheless, has the same duties as the trustee of a living trust. He must hold the assets as a fiduciary for the benefit of a beneficiary, and perform in a similar manner. He pays the income to, and uses the principal for, the benefit of the beneficiary.

Trustees can sell, lease, mortgage, borrow money, and incur expenses like any normal human being or corporation. A trustee's prime duty, of course, is to make the trust property productive. The trustee must preserve the value of this trust asset. He must use reasonable care and skill to develop the maximum income from these assets, consistent with conservative, prudent investments which are calculated to have a minimum risk. Most trustees are prevented by law from reckless speculation. They are bound by what is known as the "Prudent Investor Rule," which originates from an old lawsuit entitled "Harvard College v. Amory," back in Massachusetts, many years ago. There is no one form of investment open to trustees. They can do many things. They can purchase bonds, a select list of corporate stocks, real estate, certain first mortgages, and also invest in their so-called common trust funds; these are pooled investments in which you own a proportionate share, based upon the value of your trust in relation to the total value of the pooled assets. They are not unlike mutual funds. They are, however, better investments than most mutual funds, and cheaper to operate.

A trustee is personally liable to the beneficiaries for any loss or depreciation in the value of the trust which was caused by a breach of trust or imprudent investments. Generally speaking, you need not fear for your trust assets so long as you name the Trust Department of a full-service bank or a private trust company as trustee. If you name a friend or relative—an individual, that is—as trustee, you may need to start worrying about your trust assets. Under certain circumstances, it might be advisable that you name your spouse as a co-trustee of your trust. However, tax problems may result from this, and you must be careful.

Trusts pay taxes! They pay income taxes. They pay gift taxes. They pay real estate taxes. So you can see that a trust is, generally speaking, not strictly a money-saving device.

In many parts of the country, there are specialized financial institutions known as trust companies. If you are fortunate enough to live in a community where there is a substantial trust company, this is usually one of the best places to bring your trust business. They are, after all, specialists. Unlike most full-service banks, they do not compete with themselves for your money. In other words, in the full-service bank, the commercial section will tell you to put your assets into their (generally poor) investment known as a savings account. The Trust Department of the same bank will say you should place your assets in their division, setting up a trust. It can all be very confusing to the innocent public. Trust companies concern themselves only with proper trust management. Most of them have a minimum amount they will take into a trust, because they want your trust to be economically feasible, practical, and profitable for you as well as for themselves. Unlike most commercial banks, the trust companies will not accept trusts that are too small.

20

Trust Abuses

For many years, I believed that a living trust could be an advantage to almost anyone. Clearly, it offers fantastic advantages to those who need it. Recently, however, since the big push for living trusts, a number of my clients with them complain that the monies they pay in annual trust fees amount to substantial sums. This is true. They further complain that the fees are paid out of their income, and amount to a large slice of their income. This is also true! I reemphasize: The name of the game is money. How can you best maximize your income with the most security? It would be dishonest not to point out that if you don't need a trust—or if the only reason you make a trust is to avoid probate—the money you will pay over the years in annual trust fees, withdrawal fees, and termination fees usually greatly exceeds a probate fee.

Generally, most residents in retirement communities moved to them from other states. They do not have their old sources of information, advice, and other help. They turn to the local banker. After all, in their old town, the banker was perhaps a lifelong friend. He had integrity, and kept their personal interests in mind.

In all fields, there are people who are motivated by their interests as well as yours. Regrettably, there is abuse by some lawyers and bankers today.

There is a lot of valid trust business among the retired. There is no reason to sell everyone a trust. However, it would appear that some banks are in the business of selling trusts to every customer, especially in retirement communities. This would be fine if there were a legitimate need and everyone could afford it. But the need is not universal, and not everyone can afford such a luxury.

The new businessmen in the Trust Departments of those few banks that sell trusts irresponsibly give the impression that they analyze your position and personal needs. They reach the same conclusion every time: You need a trust! Such coincidence is difficult to accept. Add to this the fact that in many retirement communities former trust officers are now leaving the banks to set up private law practice. Their association with the banks makes them think that they will get referrals as attorneys by the new bank trust officers who are promoting trusts, and these gentlemen expect to make a fortune grinding out the same living trust forms for everyone who comes into their door.

Remember, if your only reason to set up a living trust is to avoid a probate fee, the trust has no merit. You will not save money. It is distressing, but some individuals still think that they will.

A less than responsible banker always refers you to a lawyer who never questions the banker's motivation. He does little but grind out trusts. Your needs, the costs to you, and similar concerns rarely enter his conversation. You can recognize such a trust officer quite easily. He will rarely discuss the costs of a trust with you. He will send you to the same two or three lawyers every other trust officer in such banks will send you to, even if there are many lawyers in the retirement community. As a test, you might set up three or four interviews with three or four different banks and trust officers to see if they recommend the same lawyers. If they do, there is perhaps some cause to question their motives. You might well think there is some relationship among these lawyers whom all the banks recommend, when there are so many other qualified lawyers in a community of any size. Perhaps there is a lack of commitment to your welfare. Follow the advice of these reckless few trust officers, and you might wind up with a trust you simply cannot afford. The lawyer who plays the game with these trust officers does not work for you. He still works for the bank. The bank does not pay him in money; it pays him in clients. You pay him, but he would appear to work for the bank. His prime concern would appear to be business *for* the bank in return for business *from* the bank. When you visit such a lawyer, it is, indeed, a dismal situation. Your ultimate, independent adviser, the attorney, fails you.

Many attorneys are very concerned with trust abuse. If enough people who do not need or cannot afford a trust are sold trusts, the whole area of trust law will fall into disrespect. If that happens, a most valuable estate-planning tool will be lost. Many who otherwise could benefit from a trust will become reluctant to use it. It is vital that someone occasionally say: "The Emperor isn't wearing any clothes."

SUMMARY OF PART FIVE

Two kinds of trusts should concern you. The first is a living trust (in legal terms, an inter vivos trust). The second is a testamentary trust. For your purposes and general discussion, the law relating to both is quite similar. The basic difference is that a living trust is created now, while you live. A testamentary trust is created in your will and is not activated until after your death. A living trust is grounded in contract. Thus, contract law applies to living trusts. It is a simple agreement between you and the trustee. The trustee holds your assets and does certain things for you. In return, you agree to pay. The drafting of the instrument is critical. You should place into the trust instrument itself all necessary rights and commitments. You need proper and correct advice from an independent expert to protect your position. Be suspicious of any trust officer who suggests that the bank will be happy to prepare a trust for you without charge. If you follow such advice, you will pay for the rest of your life.

Unfortunately, some trust officers, in their enthusiasm, neglect to go into detail. Have your own lawyer draft the trust instrument. You will then be well protected. If he does not do tax-estate planning, have him recommend a colleague who does.

Trusts cost money. Make certain you understand the trustee's compensation. A trust is not inexpensive. Do not create a living trust just to save a probate fee. The money you thus save is a fraction of what you will usually spend for annual trustee's fees. You should look upon the fact that a trust will not be probated as an added benefit. It should never be the only reason for a trust.

Valid reasons for creating a living trust are:

1. You are not incompetent, but just forgetful.

2. You are ill and cannot handle your financial affairs.

3. You need help to care for yourself.

4. Your assets are so complicated and your investments so varied that it is now beyond your ability to handle them.

5. You are retired and don't want to be bothered playing the market or handling investments.

6. You have a large amount of cash, and you don't want to waste it by having it shrink in a savings-and-loan account. You want it invested by an expert.

7. You want your assets to be used for the benefit of a minor child or another unknowledgeable person who does not have the ability or capacity to invest it properly and safely.

8. You seek some of the tax advantages available through trusts.

9. You want to provide security and safety for a spouse if you die.

The annual fee charged by a trustee is usually based upon the entire principal and annual income earned by the trust. This fee is a percentage of the whole. Some Trust Departments charge a fee solely on the interest or income earned by the trust and do not base their fee on the principal in addition to the income. Make sure you understand the basis of your trustee's fees. If the annual fee is based upon the entire principal plus the earned income, make certain you put only income-producing assets into the trust. It would not be prudent to put your house into the trust and pay a trustee's fee based upon the total value of the house. Unfortunately, many Trust Departments suggest that you place your house in the trust without a valid reason—other than increasing their fees. Again, check carefully with the trustee. Be certain you understand how and on what its annual fee is based.

Also, ask what it will cost you to take anything you put into the trust out of trust. Most withdrawal fees are approximately one percent. For this reason, you might begin your trust with only part of your assets, funding it slowly over a year or two. In this manner, you can see if you are happy with the trustee's performance and can live with these trust officers—if not, your cost will be less when you terminate the trust and take your assets back.

If you create a living trust, make it revocable so that you can change it, or terminate it, if you are unhappy with it. There are very few instances when one should create a living trust for oneself and make it irrevocable. (One exception might be a life insurance trust.) There are, of course, some estate tax advantages in irrevocable living trusts, but you had better receive proper advice before using that vehicle.

When you create your trust, if you have good, secure quality stocks, don't let the bank sell them and put your assets into their common trust funds. When they sell this stock, the trust will have to pay a capital-gains tax. This tax can be substantial. If your assets are questionable, by all means let the trustee change your investments. One of the valid reasons for a Living Trust is expert investment advice. Trust Departments have a great fondness for their own common trust funds. They seem to cost the banks so little to operate and manage. Make sure you need a common trust fund before you incur the capital-gains tax it necessitates. If your assets are large enough and good enough, the bank will be happy to keep your trust as a separate trust. You must, however, insist that they do this. Once again, this is a problem for the drafter of the instrument, and yet another reason why you need an independent attorney to draft the trust itself.

The testamentary trust is similar to the living trust. The main difference is that the testamentary trust does not become active until you die. There is no annual trustee's fee until the testamentary trust is activated. If your spouse cannot handle your assets, consider a testamentary trust in your will. Even if your spouse appears astute and active today, he or she might not be so a few years after you are gone.

If your assets exceed $100,000, there might be substantial estate tax savings in the use of a living or testamentary trust. The United States federal estate tax must be paid by anyone who dies and owns assets in excess of $60,000. There are various exclusions, exemptions, and legal proceedings by which the tax can be minimized. Nevertheless, the estate tax begins when your assets exceed the sum of $60,000. The tax is not abusive up to $100,000. Beyond this point, however, the tax becomes seriously abusive. If you pass the ownership of your assets directly to your spouse as a result of your death, there will be tax, first, at your death, and then once again at the spouse's death. The second tax will be much higher than the first tax. A single person does not have the deductions available to a married person. The second death tax is often enormous, and way out of proportion. You can save the second death tax by placing your assets into a trust under your will for your wife, if you don't have a standby trust.

Proper drafting is critical in all trusts. Your spouse cannot change a testamentary trust once you die. Particular care must be taken when you draft the instrument into your will. You should analyze clearly what your spouse will need in order to protect her. Your spouse should know what is going on, and must tell you if she can live with what you put into that trust. She has the same duty to tell you her needs here as in the living trust.

In my opinion, no one should ever name anyone or anything as his trustee except the Trust Department of a full-service bank or trust company. If you do otherwise, there is usually an unhappy beneficiary after your death. Mutual funds are poor trustees. They do not, as a general rule, offer valid, full-service Trust Departments. Their trusts are most impractical and overpriced.

Never, absolutely never, name your child as your trustee! It is possible that he will consider this money his before his time.

The Trust Department of your full-service bank, and particularly a trust company, are in the business of managing trusts. They understand the nature and the duties of a fiduciary relationship. They have experts analyzing the market constantly. Your child probably has a full-time job and a full-time family. The effort he will expend in your behalf may be worthless; it is a serious error to name your child as a trustee. If you have need for a trust, you deserve the services of an expert.

PART SIX
Probate-Avoidance Tools

21

The Effects and Dangers of Avoiding Probate

As already stated, the *only* way to avoid probate is to own nothing when you die. To do this, you must give everything you own away while you live.

Every probate-avoidance tool requires that you give away what you own while you live. In other words, you make someone else the owner of your assets. Those who recommend these tools should instruct you on the legal complications. They should explain the legal and tax effects, and the dangers involved. Otherwise, they mislead you. In effect, they cause you to abuse yourself.

If you do not understand the meaning of probate-avoidance tools, don't use them. You cannot protect yourself without a thorough understanding of the methods to avoid probate. When you use any probate-avoidance tool recklessly, the possibility is very strong that you will lose the ownership—and the use—of your assets while you live. Every method to avoid probate has a certain legal consequence. Each method has other and different tax consequences. You should educate yourself before you use them.

If you are advised to use joint tenancy, understand that it might delay a probate fee but incur other tax or legal consequences. If your adviser cannot explain these consequences to you, do not follow his advice.

Realtors, stockbrokers, mutual funds salesmen and clerks at banks are, unfortunately, often uninformed in the legal complications of all probate-avoidance tools, and are simply unqualified to discuss the subject. You are usually misled when you listen to them or follow their advice.

It is the uninformed who adamantly push these probate-avoidance tools on everyone in a reckless manner. A gullible public, seeking something for nothing, blindly follows bad advice.

There are three methods by which you can avoid probate. The first is by outright gift. You know what you are doing, and you actually give your assets away, now, while you live. The second is probably the most popular: Joint Tenancy with Right of Survivorship. The third is also very popular, and that is another, but really abusive, form of trust. I refer to the savings account in which you name yourself as trustee for someone else, and to the mutual fund trust, which is really not a full-service trust.

Most probate-avoidance tools cause gift taxes to vest

immediately. You, the giftor, must pay the tax. In an alarming number of cases, the probate-avoidance tools increase estate taxes, once you die. However, the worst abuse is that all probate-avoidance tools greatly restrict the use of your property and, in too many instances, you lose them while you live. Let us look at these tools.

22

Joint Tenancy with Right of Survivorship

This is, perhaps, the most well-known method to avoid probate. It really does not avoid probate; it only delays probate until the survivor dies.

Joint Tenancy with Right of Survivorship is but one of many ways in which you can hold title (ownership) to anything you own. It can be used in real estate, personal property, bank accounts, stocks, bonds, automobiles, et cetera, indefinitely. There is probably nothing that you cannot own in joint tenancy. You can be a joint owner with two, three, four, or any number of people, corporations, or other legal entities. Anyone who owns anything can hold title to it in joint tenancy with someone else.

Joint Tenancy with Right of Survivorship means that

162

each of the joint owners own everything, or 100 percent of the assets. If you own a house, and the title is in your name and the name of your spouse as Joint Tenants with Right of Survivorship, each of you owns 100 percent of the house. In other words, each joint tenant does not own 50 percent (or half a house), but you each, actually, own the entire structure. Therefore, each joint owner has 100 percent interest in the home. If the house is worth $30,000, you don't each have a $15,000 interest. Each of you has a full $30,000 interest in the whole thing. There are, however, other ways to own real estate or personal property, in which the different owners can have a different percentage of ownership. There are often tax advantages in owning a property other than jointly.

It is because of the 100 percent ownership by each joint tenant that the survivorship feature works. In other words, if each of you owned 100 percent of that house, and one of you died, the survivor, having owned 100 percent all along, simply continues to own 100 percent of the house. The same would be true, of course, with common stocks, bank accounts, or anything else. It is this survivorship feature that delays the need for probate, when the first joint tenant dies, until the last joint tenant dies. For this reason, anything that is owned in Joint Tenancy with Right of Survivorship will not be probated at the first death. The then-deceased, former joint tenant lost his interest in that property at death. This looks like simplicity itself, does it not? It is.

The simplicity is very expensive. You pay a very high price. It is often too costly.

If the deceased former joint tenant also had a will in which he also tried to give away his ownership interest in that joint property, he could not do it. Joint tenancy assets belong to the surviving joint owner. The house, the car, the land belongs to the surviving joint tenant. Joint tenant property cannot be given away by will. At the moment of death, the first joint tenant loses all of his interest. The surviving joint tenant, having owned 100 percent all along, merely becomes the sole and exclusive owner. This is a very important point. *You cannot give anything you own as Joint Tenant with Right of Survivorship away in your will.* You cannot pass a jointly-owned asset on to your children. This survivorship feature is a two-edged sword. It is probably safe to say that if you put your assets into joint tenancy, it would work to your advantage if you become the surviving joint tenant. It is for this reason that one should never use Joint Tenancy with Right of Survivorship with anyone except a husband or wife in a first marriage. A husband and wife in a first marriage have the same children, the same heirs. They also would have the same creditors, if any.

When the second or surviving spouse dies, the property will be probated. You will have, of course, delayed probate at the first death—this can be a money-saving feature, though, it is not worthwhile except in first marriages. Isn't it impractical to jointly own something with a second spouse merely to save a 4 percent probate

fee, if that spouse survives you and then owns everything? This means all of your assets along with all of
his or her assets. This is especially impractical if you
want to protect your children from a former marriage.
My colleagues and I, who practice as estate lawyers,
can tell you that in the overwhelming majority of cases,
the surviving spouse usually makes a will after the death
of the former joint owner. In that will, he or she gives
the former joint property away to his or her own children, and completely disinherits the children of the
now deceased joint owner. In other words, you might
disinherit your children if you use Joint Tenancy with
Right of Survivorship with a second spouse.

There are other reasons not to use joint tenancy.
Joint Tenancy with Right of Survivorship should rarely
be used by anyone, even a husband and wife in a first
marriage, if their total assets exceed $100,000. Serious
tax considerations apply. Everyone is subject to a federal estate tax after death. Some people are subject to
an additional state tax in the jurisdiction where they
live at the time of death. Taxes are based upon the
ownership of taxable assets. If you die and own
$100,000' worth of property jointly with your spouse or
anyone else, you each own $100,000. That property is
usually taxed at each of your deaths, so that the
$100,000' worth of property ends up being taxed twice,
or to the extent of $200,000—unless it can be proved
that there was no contribution on the part of the first
deceased joint owner so that some taxes might be saved.
Such proofs are very expensive. Generally speaking, if

a deceased joint owner owned it all, by definition, then all of it is subject to tax. For this reason, it is rarely prudent to have anything in Joint Tenancy with Right of Survivorship if your assets exceed $100,000.

If you wish to prove that all of the joint property should not be taxed to the estate of the first joint owner, you will find it possible, but very costly and time-consuming. You must prove to the satisfaction of the Internal Revenue Service that there were no contributions toward the purchase of these assets by the deceased spouse. Often these records are hard to come by, and legal fees and accounting fees unfortunately do not come cheaply. Just be aware, even if your executor knows enough to claim an exemption from tax, that your estate has the expense and extra burden of proof.

There is still another good reason not to use Joint Tenancy with Right of Survivorship. Assume that you are a widow or widower or a single person. If you take something of your own and make another person a joint tenant with you, you may be subject to a gift tax. Look at it this way: A widow owns 100 shares of AT&T. She puts her daughter's name on the stock as a joint tenant. The daughter now owns 100 percent, or 100 shares of AT&T. If she did not pay 100 cents on the dollar for this, then her mother made a gift to her. There can be no other explanation. A gift tax could vest immediately.

If a gift tax vests and is due, the giftor—the person who makes the gift—must pay the tax. In our example, the mother will have to pay the tax. In some states the tax does not vest until the gift is perfected. Some states rule that the gift vests only when any part of the asset is used by the person who receives the gift (in our example, the daughter) or is, perhaps, attached by her creditors. Other states rule that the moment you make anything joint, it becomes vested, with each joint owner actually owning 50 percent. In any event, gift taxes are not cheap. They are, however, less expensive than estate taxes. Indeed, I have often suggested that clients make gifts to their children, and then prepared gift tax returns for them. They can be used by the wealthy to minimize their estates at death, thereby saving on estate taxes. However, it is doubtful that more than 10 percent of the entire American population will receive any benefit by paying gift taxes to save estate taxes. Most of us just do not have enough money to make this practical. Gift taxes can be complicated and compounded if you make mistakes. Usually, local law will determine if there is a tax, but it is a federal tax which must be paid to Uncle Sam.

There is still another and even more dangerous reason for not using joint tenancy. Your children are different people. They have different obligations. If your child is a joint owner with you, then by definition that child, in the majority of states, owns 100 percent of your assets. If your child has any creditors, you are in trouble. The creditors of your child can take away the joint property. In a frighteningly large number of cases, creditors of children who were joint owners with parents have attached and garnished the jointly-owned property. In other words, they take away your property to pay the debts of your joint-owner. I have grieved with many widows over the fact that their bank accounts and savings accounts had been depleted or emptied by the creditors of their children.

It often appears that clerks in banks do not know enough, or do not care enough, to tell you that joint bank accounts are dangerous, and can be attached by the creditors of your joint-owner. All it takes is one auto accident. It happens every day. Lawyers and creditors' organizations know that many parents, in an attempt to avoid probate, put the names of their children on things they own. Do not think for a minute that by not telling your child about the joint account or joint stock you make yourself safe. It is naïve to do that. In this day of computers, your child's judgment creditor can check every bank account in your name in a few hours, no matter where you live. Whenever a lawyer sues someone for debt, the first thing he asks is, "Do you have any living parents?" He then checks through a creditors' organization and runs the computer list of bank accounts in that particular community where mother or father lives. If he finds the parent's name and sees that the child's name is also on the bank account, he then attaches it. It can happen within 24 hours. Why take such a risk? Don't use joint tenancy with anyone except a husband or wife in a first marriage, and then only if you have less than $100,000.

Joint Tenancy with Right of Survivorship can cost many tax dollars. These tax dollars must greatly exceed a probate fee. Such joint tenancy can also cause you to lose your assets today, while you live. It can further cause you to disinherit your children and family. Because each joint tenant owns all of the joint assets, any joint tenant can take them out of the bank and use them as he will. And, in addition, creditors of each joint tenant can attach joint property.

Never use joint tenancy with second spouses, parents, children, nieces, nephews, or friends. The few areas of practical use and possible savings through the use of joint tenancy are often outweighed by the possible loss of the assets while you live. The benefits of joint tenancy are few. The faults and misuses of it are many. The wrong use of joint tenancy can be tragic.

In reviewing some of the dangers of joint tenancy, because it is so misused and misunderstood, I have had to oversimplify. Be aware that there are exceptions, and more detailed explanations, which you should seek from your own attorney.

The following list of dangers is only partial. If you believe joint tenancy might fit your situation, you should obtain detailed advice from your own lawyer. Be sure he has some knowledge of estate planning.

Joint tenancy can, in a taxable estate, cause unnecessarily increased severe federal estate taxes. This is because joint assets are taxed twice, and at a much higher rate the second time.

You can lose your assets to the creditors of your joint owner.

Your joint assets can be used to pay the estate taxes

or debts of your joint owner, if his personal assets are not sufficient and if he dies before you.

Joint tenancy can cause you to unintentionally disinherit someone. The party you did not intend to inherit your assets sometimes becomes the eventual owner of them. Occasionally, I must tell a child that Father's or Mother's checking account or savings account belongs to a neighbor, whose name was placed on the account by the parent in the belief that the neighbor would pay his bills if he could not do it himself. At the parent's death, the account belonged by law to the surviving joint tenant—the neighbor. Thus the parent had disinherited his child.

Joint tenancy will often cause gift taxes. If the gift taxes are not paid, large interest and penalties will vest in the future.

There are three big NOs relating to joint tenancy. They are:

1. Joint tenancy does not replace a will.

2. Joint tenancy does not save taxes.

3. Joint tenancy does not protect *you* while you live.

Generally speaking, it is safe to assume that joint tenancy should only be used in the following circumstances:

1. By a husband and wife, with each in a first marriage.

2. When the total assets of both joint tenants are less than $100,000.

3. When assets were placed in joint tenancy slowly over the years, a little at a time, as they were earned.

As a final statement, let me reiterate: Joint tenancy should *only* be used between a husband and a wife in a first marriage, if everything both of you own does not exceed $100,000.

Joint tenancy clearly can be a most expensive mistake. Mutual funds salesmen and bank clerks usually are not academically qualified to discuss this subject with you.

Joint tenancy does not prevent a probate, it merely delays it until the last joint owner dies. The cost of probating the entire assets at the time the last joint owner dies can be much more expensive than two modest probates. The estate taxes, almost every time, will be greater than they would have been paid if you had not used joint tenancy. The alleged advantages of joint tenancy are greatly overrated. Unfortunately, the appearance of such a simple solution can be overwhelmingly appealing. This false simplicity, and failure to explore the meaning of joint tenancy, can cause too many people to suffer greatly.

When you place a child's name on your property and make him a joint owner with you, this is a gift. In other words, joint tenancy means each joint tenant can actually own 100 percent of the property, *right now*. If your child or joint owner did not own this property last week, be it your home, bank account, or common stock, and he owns it this week, there can be only two reasons: Either he purchased it from you and paid you full value, 100 cents on the dollar; or you gave him a gift. Unnecessary and severe gift taxes can vest immediately. Some people make multiple gift taxes by virtue of the fact that they put more than one person's name on their property. Be very careful. If you put only one child's name on the property to eliminate the multiple gift tax problem, you have disinherited your other children, if any. This child has no legal duty, subsequent to your death, to share these assets with your other children. Often, most regrettably, they do not.

The second tax abuse is in the federal estate tax loss. The federal estate tax, which is the tax on the passing of ownership at your death, is a progressive tax. In other words, the larger the amount of assets, the higher the percentage of tax. When the surviving or last joint tenant dies, everything will be taxed. Everything must, therefore, be taxed at a higher rate.

Finally, in perhaps the worst abuse of joint tenancy, the people who eventually receive your assets once you are dead may not be the people you would have chosen. Sometimes, these people receive your assets while you live. Let us look at two vicious examples.

The "clerk" at a savings institution in my community insisted that a woman put her daughter's name on her bank account. The woman told her lawyer that the clerk had insisted that this would save a probate fee, and that the clerk did not agree with her lawyer, who could not convince her that this was a dangerous thing to do. She insisted that her daughter did not know about the joint account. She also insisted that her daughter was wealthy and had no need of her money. She was sure that her daughter would never take her money, anyway. The wealthy daughter subsequently went through bankruptcy.

The trustee, in this bankruptcy proceedings, fully aware—as all lawyers are—that parents today irresponsibly place their children's names on their own assets, simply said to the bankrupt daughter: "Do you have any living parents?" The daughter said, "Yes; Mother lives in Sun City, Arizona." It took the trustee less than two days to have a computer run made on all banks and savings institutions in Sun City. He found Mother's account. The daughter's name was on the account. He immediately attached the entire bank account and took the money back East to pay off the daughter's creditors. He wiped the mother out. She sat in that lawyer's office and cried. The lawyer asked her why she did it when he had begged her not to. Her answer was, "To save a probate fee." The lawyer didn't say it, but he felt like saying, "Well, then, rejoice. You did, indeed, save a probate fee. You now have nothing to probate."

Another common and vicious abuse caused by joint tenancy was suffered by a widowed client of mine. She and her husband had owned everything in joint tenancy. The estate was not taxable, so there was good reason for it. They had a first marriage only. It was simple. She owned everything, and she thought this was beautiful. In time, she remarried. Since it was so simple the first time, she and the new he agreed to make everything joint in this, her second marriage. She died first. She had an emotionally disturbed daughter, whom she wished to protect under her will. Unfortunately, her will could not give away jointly-owned property. The assets belonged to the surviving joint tenant. Her second husband had no interest in this daughter. He disappeared with all of his money. Unfortunately, his money now included his former wife's money. The daughter is now doomed to a life in a state institution.

Many people feel that joint tenancy replaces a will. It does not! Oddly enough, there are some lawyers who also say this. It is absurd. Nothing replaces a will. You might not have everything you own in joint tenancy. You will need a will to dispose of the other things. You might be the surviving joint tenant, who owns everything. Certainly, at that point, you will need a will. Joint tenancy *never* replaces a will.

Joint Tenancy with Right of Survivorship is dangerous. Many of you can benefit from its intelligent use. You must, however, carefully decide whether or not you can afford to use it. Get proper advice from a knowledgeable source before you decide it is for you.

For those of you who can use joint tenancy (and there will be many of you), you will delay a probate fee when the first spouse dies, and until such time as the surviving spouse dies. There is an advantage to this, if it fits your needs, and you can use the joint tenancy vehicle safely. Your attorney will be in a position to analyze this for you.

Should you be a widow or widower and use one child as your joint tenant, you may nevertheless disinherit your other children, if any. At your death, your surviving joint tenant will own everything and have no duties or obligations to turn any of these assets over to your other children. Use the joint tenancy vehicle with caution.

Many people put a child's name on their bank accounts or other assets as joint tenants so that in case of illness this child can assist them, maintain them, and pay their bills. This is a human and understandable motive. It is, nevertheless, very dangerous.

There is a simple and much safer way to obtain the same protection. You can give power of attorney to any of your children. In this manner, you can keep your assets in your name alone. With the power of attorney, your attorney-in-fact (your child) can still reach all of your assets in an emergency. He can also maintain you with your money through the use of the power of attorney. Powers of attorney are explained in detail in Part Seven.

Finally, many people don't consider what will happen to their bank accounts if their joint owner dies first. It does happen, you know. If you live in a state that locks bank accounts (and most of you do), your checking account, your savings account and your time certificates of deposit will be frozen when your joint owner dies.

23

---

*The Pseudo-Trust
That Is Not a Trust*

The Part on trusts illustrated how a valid trust, with a trust company or full-service bank as trustee, might offer substantial advantages to those of you who can afford such a luxury and have such a need. Such a trust would eliminate the requirement of a probate since you, the owner, gave your assets away to the trustee during your lifetime. The valid trust vehicle serves a most useful and practical purpose. However, trusts have been sorely abused by some financial institutions, stockbrokers, and mutual funds.

Many of the aforementioned now realize that there is substantial danger in the reckless use of joint tenancy. Most of them do not understand why and show little desire to learn. And, many continue to recommend it in a most abusive fashion.

Today, they may recommend that you purchase

equities, or real estate, or place your money in a financial institution savings account, in what looks like a trust, but, in fact, is not. Today, you can open a savings account in most financial institutions in your name, as trustee for another person. Many people open such savings accounts in their names as trustee for their spouses. The spouses return the favor. Both spouses open similar trust-type accounts in their joint names as trustees for their respective children, and other members of the family. Such an account will usually read (using myself as an example): "Melvin Jay Swartz, Trustee for Beth Ames Swartz (my wife)." Mutual funds and stockbrokers sell their wares in a similar manner. This is a very dangerous thing to do.

If you recall the Part on trusts, you will remember that what you say in a trust is essentially, "I no longer am the owner of this asset. I make a gift for the benefit of the beneficiary. I give this asset away to the trustee to hold for the benefit of the beneficiary."

What you did, of course, was give this asset away during your lifetime. The same is true with most types of savings account trusts. You state, technically: "I make a gift of this savings account asset to the beneficiary, and I only hold empty legal title for the benefit of the beneficiary." The beneficiary, of course, is the owner of the important equitable title, in most instances. (There are a few minor exceptions in two or three states.) It is hardly worth the dangerous effort for you to take such chances with your money.

When you hold something as trustee for a beneficiary,

it is not in your estate for probate or the payment of your bills. This is understandable, since you no longer own it. It is for this reason that the so-called trust-type bank accounts do not require a probate at your death.

However, this is not a true trust. The trustee performs no services for the benefit of the beneficiary. Indeed, the beneficiary usually cannot reach the assets while the trustee lives. The trustee and the trustor, in this instance, are often one and the same person. This would appear to be a good and secure thing. Most financial institutions state that this is a safety feature for you, and use it as a selling point. It is exactly the opposite.

When you declare yourself trustee for anyone (child or otherwise) in these bank accounts, or stocks, or time certificates, you are often presumed by law to have made a gift to the beneficiary in that account. In the majority of states, gift taxes will vest at once and must be paid. In a few states they can vest later. Gift taxes are not cheap. They are usually more than any probate fee.

If you, the trustee, become ill, have a stroke, or are otherwise incapacitated, a serious question arises as to who can reach this money. One thing is sure: The beneficiary usually cannot. If he cannot (assuming, of course, he would want to), no one else can either. In other words, only so long as you are healthy and trustee can you yourself take the money out of the bank account or order a sale of the stock. If you are unhealthy and cannot care for yourself, in the majority of states your guardian will usually not be able to reach these assets for you.

Guardians can only reach what the ward owns for himself. Remember: You no longer own the savings account or the stock certificates. You gave those assets away when you made yourself trustee. You, as trustee, hold only the empty legal title for the benefit of the beneficiary.

There is much confusion in the law relating to this type of account. Costly lawsuits requiring court interpretation often result when uses of these accounts are disputed. Such lawsuits must, by their very nature, be expensive. You, of course, will pay for the lawsuit. If you are retired and cannot reach your savings or other assets, you could be in a most regrettable position. Wouldn't it be ghastly to have a stroke and find yourself residing in a state institution because you have given your money away through the bank accounts and cannot now support yourself? The beneficiary can't help you because he can't touch the trust account while you are alive. The retired are at an age when such things can happen to them.

Such savings accounts are not truly trusts. They are attempts on the part of financial institutions to make you think there is insurance for additional savings accounts, so that they can obtain more of your money on deposit. Such accounts are backfiring all over the country. Many of you will buy expensive lawsuits if you do this with your savings. The same thing may happen if you purchase stocks in your name as trustee for someone else.

24

The Abusive Trust

A few years ago, a mutual funds salesman wrote a book attacking the legal system. Among other things, he attempted to tell you how to avoid a terrible thing called probate.

That book stated that you can avoid probate by buying the author's mutual funds, and take title (ownership) either as Joint Tenant with Right of Survivorship, or in some of his mutual funds "trusts." Finally, it stated that you can name yourself "trustee" when you purchase a fund sold by the author.

There was nothing new in that information, but you should accept technical legal advice only from your personal attorney, who can give you information for your individual needs.

Mutual funds "trusts" are, simply, quite unlike a valid trust with a full-service Trust Department of a good bank as your trustee.

All mutual funds companies were impressed with the success of that book—and the monies made by the author-salesman from the subsequent sale of his mutual funds.

As a result, today you can purchase any mutual fund in what the fund calls a "trust." You can purchase these funds in your name, or name the fund itself as trustee.

These funds provide you with enormously dangerous trust forms without charge. Once again, the appeals of false simplicity and getting something for nothing are overwhelming. People are not told of the 8 percent commissions and many other dangers. Too many of them fall into a dreadful trap. The so-called trust forms provided by the mutual funds do not include any of the services which you would want and get from a valid trust.

A number of my widowed clients are locked into a vicious mutual fund trust, established by their late husbands. These men purchased the fund and named the fund, itself, as trustee for themselves and their wives. Now that the husbands are dead, the trusts are irrevocable. The mutual fund organization, as trustee, owns all of the assets, albeit for the benefit of the now grieving widows.

The rather dismal performance of most mutual funds over the past few years is no longer news. Most of these funds do not provide sufficient income to give the beneficiary a reasonable standard of living. Most of these trust forms do not allow for an invasion of principal on the demand of the beneficiary.

These beneficiaries are stuck with a minimum income. Should they become ill, the boiler-plate, poorly drafted forms provided free of charge by the mutual funds sales organizations do not allow a trust officer to pay bills and maintain the beneficiaries. These are vital services that any reasonable, ethical trust department of a full-service bank will provide.

The public has only slowly become aware of the disaster called a "mutual fund trust." A few such funds now worry about misleading the public. Finally! These few have amended their rigid forms and now allow for some invasion of principal in their canned trust instruments. But have you ever tried to contact a trust officer who lives 1500 or 2000 miles away from you? It is very difficult. Even those funds which allegedly allow an invasion of principal rarely provide a trust administrator to handle your account.

Your widow will be most fortunate if she can even find the alleged trust officer "in charge" of her account. These fund organizations, however "inadvertently," make it extremely difficult for your widow to reach them by long distance to invade principal to get back some of the money you placed into these "trusts." Remember that the helpful, friendly, efficient salesperson was working for a commission. He is no longer interested in helping your spouse once you are dead. He has no contact with his mutual fund organization apart from selling. You must make your contact directly with the main office of the mutual fund, and that is why it is so difficult to receive proper satisfaction from mutual fund trusts.

Mutual funds as investment organizations, or as trustees, are subject to no controls. The underworld could buy that fund and bleed it dry. On the other hand, the Trust Department of a full-service bank is constantly checked by your state and federal governments. Once again, if your trust officer is in the community where you and/or your spouse reside, you can go to his office, bang on his desk, and demand either explanations or money. You cannot do this with a mutual funds office thousands of miles away. Generally speaking, few mutual funds, in my opinion, are competent trustees. If you want a trust, don't take short cuts. Pay the money for proper legal services. Your attorney will prepare a valid trust instrument with invasion rights and many other advantages and benefits at a local full-service bank with a good Trust Department or at a trust company.

It does you or your widow very little good to avoid probate only through the loss of these assets while you or your wife lives.

25

The Worst Trust of All

Occasionally, a client walks into my office and asks me to assist in putting everything he or she owns into his or her own name as trustee with himself or herself as beneficiary. This can be an invitation to disaster. It is almost universally an invitation to expensive tax litigation.

If you are both trustee and beneficiary, then indeed, technically speaking, there are those who believe you do not have a trust. A valid trust requires that the equitable title and the legal title be split. You will recall that the trustee owns the empty *legal* title and holds the assets in trust for the benefit of the beneficiary—a different person who has the *equitable* title. If you hold both the equitable and the legal title, then you own it in every respect, regardless of whether or not you call yourself trustee. This can remove the normal trust advantages and cause a loss of tax savings.

When such an individual requests this, I question him. It is usually obvious that he wants to avoid probate and is embarrassed to say so. Recently, one married woman came into my office for assistance. She had an inadequate form which she pulled out of an inaccurate book which sold very well a few years ago. It purported to establish a trust wherein she would be trustee for herself. She wanted me to help her complete the form. I refused.

She wanted, in effect, to make herself trustee of everything, and name her son as beneficiary. She was married. She had deeds from her husband, turning all property over to her. The deeds were improperly executed. They were also taken from that same inadequate, poorly drafted book. I asked her what would happen to her husband if she died first. She assumed her son would take care of her husband. This is a very irresponsible assumption.

I asked this lady what would happen if her son died shortly after her. She didn't know. The son probably had a will giving everything to his wife.

How would you like to be living in a home you purchased and paid for and learn only after the fact that it is now owned by your daughter-in-law, who tells you to leave? This is an outrageous thing to have happen. I refused to assist this lady. She went elsewhere for help. I believe she did what she wanted to do, for she was determined to save the probate fee. The fact that she cut off her husband, perhaps causing him to land in a state institution, if she died first apparently didn't concern her.

It is the rare person indeed who can receive an advantage by naming himself trustee of his own assets, without expert help. Do not take your assets and make yourself trustee for your children and cut off a spouse. Even if you are a widow or a widower, do not put your assets in your name as trustee for your children. If you insist on naming yourself trustee of your own trust wherein you are the first beneficiary and your children are the second beneficiaries, protect yourself. Do not name your children as second or "alternate" trustee. It would not do to have yourself declared incompetent so that your children could become trustees. Play safe and at least name a full-service Trust Department of a full-service bank or a trust company as your alternate trustee if you insist on using this self-trust.

Just as I was reviewing the final portion of this Part, a gentleman walked into my office. He introduced himself, and handed me two trust forms. One was drawn by a local title company. One was drawn by a local bank. Both forms predated the 1969 tax law changes relating to trusts. He told me he wanted a trust; he asked that I help him fill out these forms. He said it shouldn't cost much money.

I tried to explain to him that his forms no longer applied because of subsequent tax changes. He would not listen.

He stated that he didn't want the trust to take effect until after he died. I told him that what he wanted was a testamentary trust, which belongs in a will. His trust forms were suggested forms for a living trust and could not do the job. He glared at me.

Finally, I pulled out a series of suggested trust forms prepared by local banks. Every full-service bank provides suggested trust forms which may be used by an expert to apply to the specific needs of the individual. I tried to tell him that all of these forms were different, that they all have different applications and tend to give too much power to the bank. Only an expert can use them properly.

He jumped up, glared at me again, and said furiously, "I have been a real estate man in this community for thirty-five years. Every time I had a lawyer involved in a deal, he blew it." With this, he walked out.

He didn't give me a chance to say, "You appear to be a foolish and, indeed, dishonest man. You want to use my services without paying for them. You will most probably dynamite your estate, bringing great expense on your children, and putting your wife in a most unfortunate position. You don't even have the intelligence to know what you are doing when you should use an expert."

No doubt, such a man, who only wants something for nothing, will fill in the forms himself. It is too bad he will not be around to see the disaster his family may suffer.

SUMMARY OF PART SIX

The only way to avoid probate is to own nothing when you die. It is important to recognize this fact.

There is no other way to avoid probate. You must give what you own away while you live to avoid probate.

All probate avoidance tools have different tax consequences and different legal consequences.

Play safe. Don't follow the advice of real estate brokers, mutual funds salesmen, savings and loan institution clerks, or bank clerks, who tell you they will save you a probate fee. They usually don't know what they are talking about. Certainly, they don't know the full tax dangers and legal complications. You might lose the use of your assets while you live, and that would be a disaster for you.

Very few of the retired can afford to lose their assets. Fewer of them, still, can replace the assets, once lost.

The bank wants your money. They will tell you how to save probate, so long as you keep your money in their bank. They are not usually concerned with the dangers to you which their methods cause. The same is true of mutual fund organizations and savings and loan institutions. Don't be naive. Altruism is not their business. They want your money. If they can help you while getting your money, fine. But the prime motivating factor is their profit, not your security. Don't take chances and lose your money when you might need it most.

There are only three basic ways to save a probate fee.

The first is by gift. You can give your assets away right now.

The second is Joint Tenancy with Right of Survivorship. There are enormous dangers when you use joint tenancy. Joint tenancy always increases your taxable estate. It can cause unnecessary and severe federal estate taxes. You can lose your assets to the creditors of your joint owner. Your joint assets can be used to pay the taxes and expenses of your joint owner, if the joint owner dies. Joint tenancy can cause you to unintentionally disinherit a relative. You can't give joint assets away by will; they belong to your joint owner. If you make them joint with one child, you may have disinherited all your other heirs. If you make your assets joint with a second spouse, you may well disinherit all your children.

Joint tenancy can cause expensive gift taxes.

Joint tenancy does not replace a will. Joint tenancy does not save taxes. Joint tenancy does not protect you while you live.

Most importantly, joint tenancy does not prevent probate. Joint tenancy merely delays probate until the last surviving joint owner dies. The cost of probating the entire assets when the last joint owner dies can be much more expensive than two modest probates.

No responsible person would put everything he or she owns into joint tenancy. Most people own something alone. A will is the best way to dispose of it. If you are a last surviving joint tenant, you own everything. You then need a will to dispose of those assets after your death.

Joint tenancy can *only* be used *safely* by a husband and wife in a first marriage, if everything both spouses own does not exceed $100,000.

The final way to avoid probate is a trust vehicle. If

you do not yet understand why, reread the Part on trusts. When you put something into a trust, you give it away while you live. You make the trustee the legal owner. This can be a very sensible and valid thing to do if you have a trust at a trust company or a full-service bank with a competent Trust Department.

Do not buy mutual funds in your name as trustee for anyone else. Do not buy a mutual fund and make the fund your trustee. It does little good for you to save a probate fee if you lose the use of these assets while you live.

Mutual funds trusts are not full-service trusts, in any sense.

Do not put your bank accounts in your name as trustee for someone else. You might lose the use of them while you live. You might pay gift taxes. Remember, once you retire you must preserve your assets. You must not take reckless chances and lose them while you live.

PART SEVEN

Common Problems, and Advice to the Retired

26

What to Do When Your Spouse Dies

When your spouse dies, you should do NOTHING. Most widows or widowers are in no condition to do anything right away. There is no emergency, and this is not the time to rush around.

Make the necessary funeral arrangements and do little else. Within a week or ten days after the funeral, you should have a conference with your attorney and then plan what must be done.

Do not make funeral arrangements alone. If a son or daughter is not available, take a friend along. Unfortunately, some funeral directors use the occasion of grief to sell elaborate trimmings. This is not the time to waste money. A modest, reasonably priced funeral is all any of us need.

Many cities through the country have societies which

193

arrange funerals. Funeral societies are often run by local churches. You need not be a member of any particular faith to join a society. Family memberships cost between $15 and $25 for life. Members are then entitled to funerals which will cost in the area of $500, $700, or $1,000, through the society's contract prices. These societies contract with local funeral directors who guarantee reasonable, efficient, competent, and honest services in good taste. Consider investigating your local funeral society.

When you make funeral arrangements for a departed spouse, you need the gentle, firm guidance of an impartial close friend. Do not subject yourself to the subtle but nevertheless high pressure of a funeral director without assistance. Try to be prudent in your choices and plans. This is not the time for extravagance, or unnecessary and elaborate expenditures.

Most states impose a tax when someone dies; These states will flag or seal any bank account or safety deposit box owned by a newly deceased depositor. You should take precautionary steps. Each spouse should have a separate bank account containing a few thousand dollars in his or her own name. You will probably not need any more than this. While you both live, you can reach the other's bank account through the use of a simple power of attorney. Every husband and wife should give each other the power of attorney.

Most states will open safety deposit boxes, and release bank accounts to a surviving spouse, as soon as they have been audited. Make arrangements with the man-

ager of the bank to audit safety deposit boxes and accounts at your earliest convenience, or as soon as local
law will allow. Your attorney will help you do these
things quickly. He will also help you obtain tax waivers,
which are required to release the money.

If your deceased spouse had a proper estate plan, the
attorney will take steps to commence the probate, if this
is necessary. He will help you obtain the release of joint
assets, if you and your spouse used joint tenancy. Once
your affairs are in order, you should continue to seek
proper legal advice. Do not take the advice of uninformed children. Do not take the advice of your neigh-
bors as it comes over the back fence. This is one time
in your life when expert advice is needed.

If you are concerned with investments, find a competent investment adviser. Do not let him or her churn
your investments by buying and selling recklessly. No
widow should speculate in the market. High income-
producing, secured investments should be sought and
then retained. These investments will slowly hedge
against inflation. Do not buy mortgages. They destroy
liquidity and can be dangerous. Do not purchase church
bonds. If you need the money, you will probably be
embarrassed to convert the bonds of your own church.

Do not put the names of any children on any of your
assets. Prepare a power of attorney for your children,
but give it to your lawyer. Ask him to keep it safe in his
office file. Do not let your children hold the power of
attorney. Even if you are one of the fortunate whose
children will not abuse your confidence, play safe.

Tell your children where the power of attorney is located. Tell your lawyer to protect you. Instruct him not to release the power of attorney to your children without checking with you to see if it is appropriate to do so. Your lawyer should verify that you are, indeed, too ill to maintain your own affairs, before releasing the power of attorney.

If you live in a retirement community, do not sell your house too quickly. The trauma of death after a long marriage is an overwhelming experience. The fewer changes you make at this moment, the better off you will be. Particularly, don't immediately go to live with children.

Many children are afflicted with a sense of obligation on the death of a parent. Their guilt for ignoring their parents in the past overwhelms them. They now insist that the surviving parent come and live with them. Don't do it. This is always a disaster. Many of my clients returned to their retirement community, after a short visit with their children. You will be nothing but a burden to each other. You will recover from the emotional trauma more rapidly in your own home than any other place. Very few people can successfully withstand both such traumatic changes: the death of a spouse, and their own removal to a different and strange environment. Stay where you are for a while.

In time, if you wish, sell your home and move into a smaller place. However, do not rush. If you go to live with children, lease your home. My own experience would suggest that you will probably move back.

Once your affairs are in order, and your will has been checked by your lawyer, try to lead a normal life. You have friends. Spend time with them. Try to keep busy. Continue your normal activities. Do not mope around the house alone. It is important that you keep active. Leave your husband's name in the telephone book, or list your telephone in the name of your husband and yourself. If you want it in your name alone, use your initials. There are people who take advantage of widows' listings. If you live alone, without a close neighbor, you might buy a dog. A dog can be wonderful for one who is alone.

When you visit the bank, uninformed tellers and clerks will advise you to put your children's names on your various holdings and bank accounts. *Ignore* their advice. Do not put another person's name on your assets. You can well do without gift tax problems or loss of your assets to creditors of your children.

Many widows and widowers give their assets away. I feel that no one who has less than $150,000 can afford to give his principal to his children. You want to live on your income and preserve your principal. If you deplete your principal with gifts to your children, you will not be able to live on the income. This will force you to use your principal and lower your standard of living. Remember, once you give an asset away, you do not usually get it back. Don't be too quick to pay the debts of your children while you live. The best thing you can do for your children is remain independent. You would not wish them to have to support you.

Keep your assets. And keep them in your own name.

Some people run to empty a safety deposit box as soon as a spouse dies. Don't. Even if you *can* do this, because the bank has not had time to flag the box, it is dangerous. You will invite trouble. When the Internal Revenue Service audits the box, their auditors check back records to see when it was last entered. They will assume you took items of value and demand an accounting. This can be very difficult or, at best, embarrassing for you.

When anyone dies with $60,000 or more, a United States federal estate tax return must be filed on behalf of the deceased. This includes all joint property and, often, all insurance. A good percentage of people are subject to such a tax.

A married person who dies will pay no estate tax unless he dies owning assets which exceed $120,000, because of "The Marital Deduction," which allows half of a deceased spouse's estate to pass to the surviving spouse free of tax (unless an improper and poorly drafted will destroys the marital deduction, which it can certainly do).

Nevertheless, the law states that an estate tax return must be filed for assets of $60,000. If an expert tells you your spouse's estate is over $60,000 but less than $120,000, you are probably safe not to file the return. The procedure is quite costly.

Penalties and interest are due Uncle Sam if you do not file a timely return. However, if the estate of your spouse is less than $120,000, it pays no tax. And penalties must be based on the tax that was not paid. No tax means no penalties. Why waste your time and money filing a return when no tax is due?

27

The Second, or Companionship, Marriage

Twelve years in a retirement community has convinced me of the value in a subsequent marriage. This does not mean I think you should dash out and seek a new spouse. However, if good fortune blesses you and you meet a potentially congenial companion, why try to avoid it?

In time, especially if you live in a retirement community, you may want to date. Don't become overwhelmed by romance. Be cautious.

If you date someone, the two of you might become serious. This is fine. Spend time together. Get to know each other well. Analyze the character, traits, drinking habits, and the financial position of a prospective second spouse If you do all of these things, and both of you feel that a marriage could work, why not seriously consider it?

Discuss your mutual assets. You should honestly tell each other what you own. Feel free to discuss normal wishes to protect your respective families. Agree on a premarital contract, which is explained in the following chapter.

Talk about pooling your incomes, but do not make any of your assets joint in any way whatsoever. Each of you should retain exclusive and sole ownership of your own assets.

This is essential. I must repeat it. *Do not make anything you own into joint tenancy with a second spouse.*

Carefully check each other's health. You should both have a thorough physical examination. Talk to each other's physician for a mutual appraisal of your respective conditions. There is no reason for either of you to become a nursemaid to the other. Make sure your prospective spouse is in reasonably good health.

You should visit each other's children. Do not be embarrassed to discuss the potential marriage with your children. If they love you, they will understand your need for companionship. Most children will immediately worry about your disinheriting them. Don't be shocked. This is human nature. You can relieve their fears by telling them that you are going to sign a premarital contract, which will protect your assets. Tell them you intend to keep sole and exclusive ownership of your assets and will not put your new spouse's name on anything you own. Don't let them convince you to put their names on what you own.

Some children become outraged. They will still fear the loss of your assets, though they may well say that *your* happiness is the main reason for their opposition. They will reaffirm loyalty to their deceased parent. This is sad. But it should not offend you. At this stage of your life, you should be a realist. Usually, it is only the widow or widower with a former happy marriage who cannot live alone, which is, after all, a tribute to the first spouse. This is why many second marriages take place quickly. If your first marriage was a disaster, you might well not want to marry again. If you had a long, happy first marriage, you will probably want to marry a second time.

The intended couple must discuss where they will live after marriage. This is especially important if each has a home. If one spouse sells and moves into the house of the other, some protection is necessary. The spouse who owns the house of residence should change his or her will and allow the new spouse a lifetime use of the home. This is a simple procedure, and any attorney can thus alter the will for you.

Once a widow remarries, she can lose her deceased husband's Social Security. If you have your own Social Security, you will not lose this by marrying again. If your Social Security depends solely and exclusively on that of your late husband, this might (but does not always) terminate with your new marriage.

In most states, a subsequent marriage after your will is executed (signed) revokes that old will as your assets pertain to your new spouse. In other words, your new spouse will be in a position to inherit from you, as if you had died without a will. If your state statute gives a certain percentage to a spouse not mentioned in a will, your new spouse might receive money under that statute. It is for this reason that *each* of you *must* make a new will after your remarriage. In the will, you should state that this is a second marriage and that you have signed a premarital contract. You should state that, for this reason, you leave no assets to your new spouse. Once again, this is a simple procedure and any competent estate planner can handle it for you.

It is appalling how often clients come into my office, with a new spouse, to convert their assets into joint tenancy. In most cases, I am successful in preventing such nonsense. Occasionally, a righteously indignant new spouse tells me there is no danger, for they are going to make a will and divide everything between both families. It sounds nice, but it rarely happens.

Only the uninformed will make his or her accounts and assets joint with a second spouse. There are serious gift tax consequences, but there are also other considerations. Reread the chapter on joint tenancy and be aware that all the dangers explained therein apply to the second marriage. Do not use joint tenancy on any of your assets with a new spouse. Keep all of your assets in your own name.

Recently, a widow of a second marriage came to my office. I remembered her well. She had been most righteously indignant when I had insisted that her late husband, my former client, not make his assets joint with her after their second marriage. She was the one who had said that they were certainly going to divide everything, under their wills, between both families. I had reminded both of them at that time that wills can be changed. She would not hear of it. They made their assets joint. Now she was in my office, before going to her husband's funeral. She wanted an emergency codicil, right then, while she waited. She wanted to give everything she owned (which now included all joint property, most of which had belonged to her now deceased second husband) to her own children. In effect, she disinherited the children of my late client. I prepared such a codicil. If I hadn't, another attorney would have. She owned the property, since she was the surviving joint tenant. It was her right to do with it as she wished. Such inequity happens daily. Don't convert your assets into joint tenancy with a second spouse. If you do, and you die first, you disinherit your children.

28

The Premarital Contract

The following is an example of a short-form Premarital contract. Such a contract signed by a man and woman before their second marriage is the only efficient and practical way to protect their children or other heirs.

The following form is offered only as an example of what can be done. There is a variety of uses and reasons and types of marital contracts. One should not prepare a Premarital Contract without competent legal advice. Each party to the contract should have his and her own lawyer. Check it out carefully.

PREMARITAL CONTRACT

THIS AGREEMENT, dated the _____ day of _____,
19___, by and between _____(Your Name)_____,
a widow and ———————————————————, a widower
[or a single person or a divorced man], is executed in the
County of _____, State of _____, and

shall be bound and interpreted by the laws of the State of
_____ [The State where you reside]. This agree-
ment shall apply to all assets of both parties, wherever located,
and shall include after-acquired property.

The consideration for this agreement is the mutual promise
of marriage between the parties, wherein they both promise
to the other to intermarry in the very near future. If the parties
do not marry one month from date of this agreement, this
agreement shall be null and void.

Each party has heirs by a former marriage, and each party
has assets which are the sole and separate property of each
party. There will be no community or joint property owned by
the parties, since neither party will be gainfully employed subsequent to the marriage.

The parties hereto agree as follows:

1. Each has been fully informed as to the other's assets
   and property.
2. That all of the assets of _____ which
   are her sole and separate property at the time of the
   marriage and any and all accumulations thereon will
   remain her sole and separate property.
3. That all of the assets of _____ which
   are his sole and separate property at the time of the
   marriage and any and all accumulations thereon will
   remain his sole and separate property.
4. That during the continuation of the marriage and while
   the parties are living together as husband and wife,
   _____(Man's name)_____ will be the family provider and
   will adequately support himself and his wife. Since both
   parties are now retired, they will pool their joint incomes to be used for their maintenance.
5. Should the parties separate or this marriage terminate
   other than by the death of one of the parties, neither
   party will have any claim upon the other for support,
   alimony, or assistance, nor will either party have the
   right to claim against the property of the estate of the
   other in any manner whatsoever.
6. Upon the termination of this marriage by death of either

party, the survivor agrees to make no claim whatsoever against the property of the decedent nor against his or her estate; the survivor hereby waives the right to dower, curtesy or homestead rights against the estate or assets of the other except insofar as the deceased person has specifically provided for the surviving party by his or her will or by some form of joint or mutual ownership of assets or by insurance or some similar device.

7. Except as either party may intentionally cause his or her assets to pass to the survivor during his or her lifetime, upon his or her death, each party agrees to waive and hereby does waive any and all rights and interests or claims by way of inheritance, descent, distribution, family allowance, or use of home or claim of community property in the estate of the other. Each party waives all rights against the assets of the other which may hereafter be acquired by either party from his or her sole and separate property.

8. Each party specifically reserves the right to dispose of his or her own property by Last Will and Testament. Notwithstanding any of the foregoing portions of this agreement, should the survivor of the parties hereto be a beneficiary under the Last Will and Testament of the other, or as a result of insurance or joint ownership or other form of passage of property upon death, the foregoing will not bar the survivor from receiving that which he or she is specifically authorized to receive.

9. It is anticipated that the parties to this marriage will file a joint income tax return. This is in no way to be interpreted as making the assets of the parties to this marriage joint.

10. Should the parties once married elect to file a joint income tax return, it shall not be considered in any way an attempt to combine or co-mingle their assets.

This agreement is made in contemplation of marriage with the knowledge that a confidential relationship between husband and wife, and a prospective husband and prospective wife, requires utmost good faith and a high degree of fairness. It is thusly the parties hereto enter into the Prenuptial Agreement, not acting under fraud, duress, or undue influence.

IN WITNESS WHEREOF, the parties hereto have signed this instrument at the place and date first above written.

_____
(Signature)

_____
(Signature)

This agreement must be signed before a notary public by each of you, to have any validity.

29

Power of Attorney

Many retired husbands and wives should give each other a power of attorney while they are both healthy. In a first marriage, it is a cheap, efficient, practical, safe, and prudent vehicle.

It works this way. If you give a power of attorney to your spouse, this makes your spouse your "attorney-in-fact." With a general power of attorney, you authorize your spouse to reach any of your assets and sign your name on legal documents if for any reason you cannot do so.

Many illnesses plague the retired. You might be unable to sign your name. You might not be able to talk, as the result of a stroke. You might not be able to walk over to the bank and take out your own money. All of these things can be done for you through a power of attorney, which can save enormous sums of money and the trauma of court guardianship. It is unsafe and imprudent to give a power of attorney to a stranger or a friend. Any lawyer can prepare a power of attorney for you. It is a very inexpensive legal document.

Once again, this form is offered only as an example. There is a variety of forms and they should only be prepared by an attorney to fit your specific needs.

A power of attorney will often read as follows:

POWER OF ATTORNEY

I, the undersigned, do by these presents, make, constitute, and appoint _____ my true and lawful attorney. Said attorney shall collect and receive all sums of money, debts, interest, insurance proceeds, dividends, and annuities whatsoever, as are now or may hereafter become due, owning, or payable to me; said attorney shall take all lawful means, in my name, or otherwise, for the recovery of the same. My attorney shall further execute, in my name, receipts, releases, and satisfactions of every kind; I further authorize my attorney to enter into my safe deposit box, located at _____ and to sell my real estate or sign all deeds, mortgages, releases, agreements, escrow instructions, notes, contracts, conveyances, and orders with regard to said real estate. My attorney-in-fact is further authorized to sell, negotiate or transfer any of my securities, equities, bonds or treasury obligations.

My attorney can write checks or withdraw any monies from savings accounts or time certificates of deposit on my behalf.

My attorney shall be entitled to do all of the aforementioned in my name as I might or could do if personally present, and I hereby ratify and confirm all that my said attorney shall lawfully do or cause to be done by virtue of these presents.

IN WITNESS WHEREOF, I have hereunto set my hand, this ____ day of _____, 19___.

_____
(signature)
(your name typewritten)

In some states you can have a durable power of attorney, which means the power of attorney will not become invalid if you become incompetent. Thus, you save the expense of court guardianships. If you live in such a state, the following paragraph should be inserted before the "In witness" clause:

This power of attorney shall not become void due to the incompetency of the grantor.

This short form power of attorney will be enough to protect you. It can be used no matter where you live. It should be notarized and signed by you before a Notary Public. You can revoke your power of attorney while you live and are competent. In most states, incompetency and death will automatically terminate a power of attorney.

The form power of attorney is presented here as a guide to enable you to better understand your attorney's explanation. It is not my desire to suggest that you prepare any legal document yourself. They can be tricky and can cause expensive problems. Any legal document should be prepared by your personal attorney.

30

Social Security and the Retired

Social Security offices in every community are staffed with competent personnel, who are agreeable and happy to assist you with any problems without charge. For this reason, a complete analysis of Social Security here is unnecessary. However, there are certain common problems that most retired people have with Social Security.

A very common problem relates to whether or not the retired person should take early Social Security. At the time this book is written, the earlier age is 62, and the later age is 65. The basic problem appears to be the degree of your loss or gain. To find this out, compute your Social Security at the younger age, and then compute it at the later age. See what you gain in the three years of early Social Security, and then decide how many years after the later age it will take you to receive enough at the larger payment rate to catch up and equal what you could have already received from early Social Security.

All things being equal, early Social Security can pay off. On the other hand, if you are at the peak of your earning potential, your Social Security benefits might increase. Thus, there is a distinct advantage to take Social Security at the later age, unless you have a medical reason for early retirement.

Because of the limits on what you can earn while on Social Security for the first decade, it is necessary to coordinate early retirement with early Social Security. Some important considerations to early retirement are the following:

1. Have you been at your present earning level long enough to receive full value from the company pension or profit-sharing plan? Most plans usually use your last five years' salary to compute your benefits. Check with the director of your company plan, and see if you have been at your present salary long enough for it to be used to determine your benefits.

2. Do you or your dependents need the continuing group medical coverage that you often lose with retirement?

3. Does your family need the company group life insurance benefits you will lose with retirement? Company policies usually start to decrease after one to three years of your retirement, and level off at about 25 percent of your original coverage.

4. If your spouse is in poor health and has a limited

life expectancy, you might work until you know if it would be better for you to take 100 percent of your retirement benefits or less, and leave a "carryover" annuity for your spouse, should you die first.

The most common problem relates to proving your qualifications for Social Security. These include:

1. Proper proof of your age.

2. Proper proof of marriage.

3. Proper proof of Social Security contributions throughout your employment.

If you don't have any of these records, you should visit your local Social Security office now, even if you cannot qualify for benefits today. Ask for a list of what they will accept in lieu of the missing proof or papers, and make plans to obtain that information while you have time. Don't wait to qualify until after you retire, when you need your Social Security. It is prudent to take steps before retirement to obtain the proper records.

If you cannot find or replace a birth certificate, there are acceptable alternative methods to establish your age. Here are some of them:

1. An affidavit from friends or relatives who can attest to the fact that they knew your parents, and were alive at the time of your birth and were aware of your birth, and that you were born at a certain place on a certain date.

2. The birth records of your physician or hospital.

3. Baptismal or early school records.

4. Registration for military service.

5. Driver's license or voter registration records.
6. Fraternal or union membership records.

Social Security benefits can also be affected by faulty work or earnings records. Everyone should check with his local Social Security office prior to retirement. Ask someone there to run a check on your Social Security earnings records. If you find an error, right then is the time to commence necessary corrective procedures.

Proof of marriage can also be a problem. Various Social Security benefits for widows require proof of marriage. The best proof is the marriage certificate. If you don't have it, and cannot replace it with a certified copy, there are, again, alternative proofs. If you are divorced, your divorce decree can be used as proof. Affidavits from friends and relatives who were at your marriage can be used. Your attorney will assist you in preparing the proper affidavits and securing the certified records.

It makes good sense to inquire in advance at your local Social Security office to see if you qualify for benefits. Many people are not insured under Social Security because of the nature of their previous work. Others don't qualify because they have not worked enough. In many instances, a small amount of part-time work for a very short period of time could qualify a retired spouse for some Social Security payments. Generally speaking, in order to qualify for Social Security, you must be what is considered a "retirement insured individual." This means that you must have a certain minimum amount of work quarters during your working career.

Important things to remember about Social Security and the retired include the following:

1. You will need birth certificates or adequate birth records.

2. You will need proper marriage records.

3. Don't wait until you retire to check on your basic benefits.

4. You should consider in advance whether to take Social Security at the early age or the later age. There is a point when additional work will not increase your Social Security benefits. You might well inquire of your Social Security office to see if you have reached this point.

5. Some wives qualify for Social Security benefits as a result of their own work, and as a result of a deceased husband's Social Security. Such a person cannot receive two benefits. She should make application for the higher. Again, the Social Security investigator who interviews you will help you determine the higher amount. Widows should retain their husband's Social Security records as proof. Some widows over the age of 60 can still receive some portion of their former spouse's Social Security, even if they remarry.

6. Federal employees are not covered by Social Security, but are covered by the United States Civil Service Retirement Act.

7. Railroad workers are protected under the Railroad Retirement Act, which is similar but not quite the same as Social Security.

8. Military personnel and civilians are covered by

different areas of Social Security. Some military personnel who have had two careers may qualify for the military equivalent to Social Security, and receive a second Social Security payment as a result of their subsequent work. Application should be made for both if you think you can qualify.

9. The present maximum death benefit available under Social Security is $255. It can be less. Not everyone is entitled to a death benefit. The death benefit belongs to a surviving spouse. There seems to be some misunderstanding that it must be paid to a funeral director. This is untrue. The surviving spouse is the one person who can demand and receive the death benefit, regardless of who pays the funeral bill.

31

Reading Materials of Special Interest for the Retired

The United States Government Research Development and Procurement Activity Department produces selected publications of interest to the public. Many of these publications are free. Those others which aren't are most inexpensive. A substantial number of them are of great value to the retired.

These publications discuss appliances, automobiles, budget and financing, clothing, fabric and laundering, consumer protection and education, food, diet and nutrition, health, cigarettes and alcohol, housing, buying, financing, home safety, heating and cooling systems, landscape gardening and pest control, recreation, travel, and other matters of consumer interest.

Write for a list of these publications to: Consumer Product Information, Public Document Distribution Center, Pueblo, Colorado 81009. They will send it to you without charge.

Of particular interest to the retired will be such publications as the following:

1. "Budgeting for the Retired Couple"(10¢). This booklet discusses planning a retirement budget, and includes a cost-of-living comparison for retired couples living in selected cities.

2. "Planning for the Later Year" (35¢). This is a comprehensive guide for retirement planning, with discussions of income, health, maintenance, housing, and some legal problems, along with the use of leisure time.

3. "Your Social Security"(30¢). This discusses eligibility, amounts of payments, and how to apply for Social Security and medicare benefits.

4. "Protection for the Elderly" (no charge). This explains how to help elderly persons protect themselves from common frauds, and details procedures for reporting such frauds to the Federal Trade Commission.

5. "Family Food Budgeting" (15¢). Discusses food plans for adequate diets at four income levels.

6. "Food Guide for Older Folks" (20¢). Written for persons over 60 years of age, this includes information on meal planning, buying, and preparing food to assure adequate nutrition.

7. "Adult Physical Fitness" (35¢). A graduated fitness program for adults who have not exercised regularly for a period of years.

8. "Hearing Aids" (60¢) offers comparative government brand-name testing and a discussion of the selection, maintenance, care, and causes of hearing loss.

9. "Back to Work After Retirement" (60¢). A fascinating discussion of specific job opportunities for retirees with help in preparing a resumé, writing a letter of application, and interviewing, plus hints on qualifying for jobs through government and private programs.

There are various pamphlets relating to nursing homes and nursing home care with checklists as to what you should look for in different homes.

SUMMARY OF PART SEVEN

When your spouse dies there is no need to do very many things immediately.

Make necessary funeral arrangements, but don't do it alone; take a relative or friend with you. At that time, you need the gentle, firm guidance of an impartial close friend. Don't subject yourself, without help, to the subtle but nevertheless high-pressure salesmanship of some funeral directors. Be prudent in your choices and plans. This is not the time for extravagance or elaborate and unnecessary expenditures.

Most states flag a bank account or safety deposit box when an owner dies. If you live in such a state, prepare now. Each spouse should have a small, separate bank account in his or her own name for emergency purposes. Most states will open safety deposit boxes and release bank accounts to a surviving spouse as soon as the assets have been audited. At your earliest convenience, make arrangements with your local bank for an audit.

Do not put the names of any children on your assets. Give your child a power of attorney, but keep the power of attorney document in a safe place. Don't give it to a child to hold. Let your lawyer hold it, and instruct him when and to whom he should release it.

Many children will insist that the new widow or widower live with them. Don't necessarily do it. This is often a disaster. You may be a burden to each other.

The death of a longtime spouse is an overwhelming trauma. Don't add to it by changing your environment too quickly. You will probably recover faster, and regain your equilibrium earlier, in your own environment with your regular friends.

Leave your telephone listing in your and your spouse's name. There are predators who look for widows' listings.

Don't buy anything from a door-to-door salesman. Don't make investment choices, or change your assets, without competent advice. You probably would do well not to attend any of the so-called "investment seminars" that are pushed daily in most retirement communities. Work only with competent brokers who come well recommended.

Reread the Part on probate-avoidance tools. Pay particular attention to the joint tenancy section and the various bank-type trust savings accounts. They are dangerous. They can cause you to lose your assets. Don't put a child's name on anything you own unless you want to lose your independence. In many cases, if you do, you will lose your assets.

Check with a tax-trained attorney to see if you must file a federal estate tax return for your late spouse's assets.

Don't rush into a second marriage. If you meet a potentially good companion, spend time together. The second or companionship marriage has many wonderful advantages. But enter into it only after serious considerations. Before remarriage, be sure to sign a premarital contract prepared by your attorney.

Never place your assets into a joint relationship with a new spouse. There are gift tax problems. Never use joint tenancy with a second spouse. You will lose control of your assets. The creditors of a new spouse could take your assets away. Play safe. Each of you should keep your own assets in your own names. Remember, you cannot give away joint tenancy assets by will. They belong to your joint owner. If you die first, they will belong to your new spouse. You may well thus disinherit your children. Be careful. Get proper advice. Use your own attorney. Your spouse's attorney might inadvertently neglect to warn you of all dangers to you.

You must redo and re-sign your will after a second marriage (in most states). Be careful here. Your old will might be revoked in relation to your new spouse. Once again, check with your own independent counsel.

The second marriage can be a wonderful thing. It usually works well in most retirement communities. When it does not work, consider annulment proceedings rather than divorce. If you can get an annulment, the wife will become once again the widow of her first husband and often regain her Social Security. She cannot do this if she gets a divorce. There are other advantages to an annulment. Check them carefully with your own lawyer.

Every retired person can benefit from one piece of advice: *Don't try to get something for nothing.* Free advice is often useless. Cheap advice often backfires. You cannot afford to lose your assets. Stop worrying about your future. Protect yourself, and your future will be secured.